THE POPES

The lives of the pontiffs through 2000 years of history

D1350305

TEXT BY
Antonino Lopes

Photo by: Gianfranco Crimi

FUTURA EDIZIONI

Original title: "I Papi"

Translation from the italian by Charles Nopar

The photographs of the popes have been
taken from the mosaics in the Basilica of San Paolo

Cover photograph: a mosaic in the Basilica of San Peter

© 1997. FUTURA EDIZIONI
00156 ROMA - Via Costantino Mortati, 130
Tel. 06/41219156

PRESENTATION

The Pontifical Administration, which has tutelage over the Patriarchal Basilica of St. Paul, has sponsored the present publication with the intent of making known the works of artistic and historical value conserved there.

The aim of this book is to give due attention to the one special feature that distinguishes the Pauline temple from all other churches: the complete series of medallions painted in oils and then turned into mosaics which depict the faces of the Supreme Pontiffs who, from Peter until the present pope, have successively guided the Church.

The pilgrims who visit the basilica have always indicated a lively curiosity in this particular series of tondos whose position above the first order of the naves and the transept do not permit them to be easily seen.

The volume, drawn up with scholarship, offers the interested reader a historical profile of each pope along with his portrait and coat-of-arms.

It is to be hoped that this publication, intended for the common reader, will help give a better appreciation of the treasures contained in the Pauline complex on the Via Ostiense in Rome, which the United Nations Organization has declared to be "a heritage of universal value".

From the sacred temple, which is named for and hands down the memory of the Apostle of the Peoples, the incomparable physician to the mystical body of Christ which is the Church, will be transmitted an ever deeper knowledge of that Church, its institutions and its saints.

1. PETER, ST.

Simon, called "Cepha" (Aramaic) or "Rock" (Pietro in Latin) by Jesus himself, was from Bethsaida in Galilee. With this name Jesus designated him as the solid foundation of the Church. A fisherman by trade, Jesus turned him into a "fisher of souls" giving him the authority to "bind and to loosen" and putting into his hands "the keys of the Kingdom of Heaven". Salvation, which Jesus brought to the world, passes from Peter to his successors and then to the Church. And finally, Christ entrusts his flock to him to be fed. This primacy of Peter has always been readily accepted since ancient times by all the Fathers of the Church even though there have been discussions and dissenting opinions. Peter presided over the first Council in Jerusalem (49) where a lively debate took place with St. Paul and it was proclaimed that salvation through Jesus was also intended for the gentiles (pagans) and thus preaching should also be made to them and not only to the Jews. The teachings of Peter, which are his recollections of Jesus, have been handed down in the Gospel according to St. Mark. In his own hand he wrote a letter to the first Christians exhorting them to live saintly lives in the midst of the gentiles and to follow the example of Jesus in suffering and persecution. A second letter was attributed was to him, but it is almost certainly not genuine even though the words and ideas could be his. His presence in Rome and his martyrdom have been attested by many fathers: Irenaeus, Clement, Alexandrinus, Ignatius of Antioch... Origen reports that Peter was martyred in Nero's time, crucified head downwards. He was buried on the Vatican hill beside the circus of Caligula and Nero on the spot where the basilica dedicated to him now stands. In the past doubt has been cast more than once on the fact that the grave over which Constantine built the basilica is truly that of the Apostle Peter. Recent archeological studies have shown with scientific rigor the truth of the tradition in which the Church has always believed: that is, that Peter indeed rests beneath the Vatican basilica.

2. LINUS, ST. (67-76)

Born in Volterra, he was bishop of Bésanconon. He was the first to take up the inheritance of St. Peter in a church that was still clandestine and in the process of formation. He opposed the doctrine of Menander, a disciple of Simon Magus who fought Christianity by denying it miraculous powers. Possibly he named the first fifteen bishops who administered the sacraments and had authority over several Christian communities. Presbyters and deacons helped the bishops in performing the sacred functions and aiding the poor. He made dispositions for women to be admitted to the holy places and attend the functions with their heads covered. It was during his pontificate that the Evangelists Mark and Luke were martyred (70 A.D). He was buried beside St. Peter in the first Vatican burial spot. It is certain that he did exist while some have thrown doubt on his election to the pontificate. In fact Tertullian maintains that Cletus and not Linus was the successor of St. Peter.

3. CLETUS or ANACLETUS, ST. (76-88)

He was born in Rome on the Esquiline hill. The two names refer to the same person. The error persisted for centuries, but the equivocation has by now been cleared up. Under his pontificate Domitian unleashed the second persecution against the Christians because they refused to contribute to the reconstruction of the Temple of Jove which had been destroyed by fire. He made dispositions for the consecration of bishops and dictated the norms for ecclesiastical dress, prohibiting them from letting their beards and hair grow. He had a small chapel built over the tomb of St. Peter which was the nucleus on which Constantine erected the first great basilica in 324 dedicated to the prince of the apostles. Cletus died a martyr in the year 88 and was buried beside St. Peter.

4. CLEMENT I, ST. (88-97)

Clement was born in Rome in the vicinity of the Colosseum. He was among the first to be baptized by St. Peter. Under the emperor Nerva the Christians enjoyed a peaceful period. Things changed under Trajan who considered Christianity to be the plague of humanity. However he did not openly persecute the Christians but ordered them to be condemned whenever they should be denounced. Clement, a strong and authoritative personality, began to arouse diffidence. Nerva had him exiled to Pontus (97) where he continued his evangelizing. A few years later, in Trajan's times, he was ordered to make sacrifices to the gods. On refusing, he was condemned to death. It was the year 100. The story goes that Clement was thrown into the sea with an anchor around his neck, but his body was miraculously retrieved and buried in the Crimea. By order of Nicholas I (858) Saints Cosmas and Damian brought his body back to Rome and had it buried on the site where the basilica bearing his name now stands. Clement was the one to introduce the liturgical vestments into the sacred functions and the use of the word *Amen*. He appointed seven notaries, one for each ecclesiastical area of Rome, to edit and file all information regarding martyred Christians. He can be considered the first pope to have abdicated, even if this was due to outside force.

5. EVARISTUS, ST. (97-105)

Born in Jerusalem of Jewish parents who had him educated at Antioch in Greece. He substituted for Clement for three years during his exile in the Crimea, after which he was elected pope.

The Christian community was growing and so it was necessary to subdivide it so as to govern it better. Thus the parishes or *tituli* were created headed by elderly priests who were later called cardinals (hinges of the organization). This may have been the origin of the Sacred College. He also instituted a group of seven deacons whose job it was to write down the popes utterances so as to avoid disputes about what he had said. The complete compendium of the truth had not yet been perfectly codified and there was constant need of corrections and rectifications. Evaristus was martyred in 105 and buried, according to tradition, near to St. Peter.

6. ALEXANDER I, ST. (105-115)

Born in Rome in the San Lorenzo quarter, he was a cultivated and enlightened person, a disciple of Plutarch and Pliny the Younger. Apparently he was only twenty years old when elected pope. On this occasion the election system was used and not the hereditary designation of master to disciple. His missionary activity must have been important and incisive since several illustrious converts are attributed to him: the prefect of Rome Hermetus and all of his family, because of which he was arrested; the tribune Quirino, his daughter Balbina and many other weighty personages. He modified and enlarged the mass, instituted the use of holy water in sacred places and houses, and he prescribed that the host be made of unleavened dough. He was martyred in Via Nomentana and buried in the church of St. Sabina.

7. SIXTUS I, ST. (115-125)

Born to the Elvidia family in Rome, he continued the work of his predecessors in organizing the ecclesiastical structure. He established that before taking charge of his seat, a bishop had to show a letter of authorization signed by the pope. He sent Bishop Pellegrino to Gaul to evangelize in certain areas not yet sufficiently influenced by Roman civilization. He set norms for several rites of the mass and ordered that holy furnishings be touched only by priests. To him are attributed the following: the triple chant of *Sanctus* during the mass; two apocryphal letters bearing on the doctrine of the Holy Trinity and the primacy of the Church of Rome. Several divergences with the Asian church go back to his papacy. After his martyrdom he was buried beside St. Peter by order of Paschal I. A thousand years later the Counts of Alife of Benevento asked to have his remains returned. Innocent II (164) granted the request. It is told that during the trip the mule carrying the urn would go no further after reaching Alatri. The people of this town accepted the holy remains and buried them on their acropolis where they are preserved to this day.

8. TELESPHORUS, ST. (125-136)

Born in Calabria of a Greek family, for many years he led the life of a hermit. He was elected pope at a time when many heresies were circulating in Rome. The most dangerous of these was the Gnostic heresy which had been spread by Valentinus in twenty years of preaching. It was founded on the idea that to conceive of the divine in an ever purer manner it was necessary to represent it as totally separate from man and the world as God was from the abyss. Magical rites in the style of Simon Magus accompanied this idea. St. Telesphorus continued the work of organizing the Church by setting certain norms. He prescribed fasting and penance in the seven weeks before Easter, thus initiating a practice that is still alive in the Christian world. He established that on Christmas Eve priests could say three masses and he introduced the *Gloria in excelsis Deo*, which he himself may have composed, at the beginning of the mass. After his martyrdom he was buried in St. Peter's tomb.

9. HYGINUS, ST. (136-140)

Born in Athens, he was considered a philosopher and he behaved like one during his pontificate, above all in the fight against the Gnostics. He had to fight particularly hard against Cerdo who denied the validity of the Old Testament and part of the Gospel according to St. Luke. He made several dispositions regulating the forming of a hierarchy among priests which was necessary due to the spreading of the Christian community. During the baptism of children, he ordered the presence of a godfather or godmother who would guide and instruct them in leading a Christian life. He ordered that churches should be dedicated. His pontificate was marked by persecutions and his martyrdom probably took place during one of these. He was buried near the tomb of St. Peter's.

10. PIUS I, ST. (140-155)

Born at Aquileia in Friuli, his was a long pontificate for those days. Some historians attribute to him the choice of the date for the celebration of Easter as the first Sunday after the March full moon. Other historians attribute this to his successor St. Anicetus. He opposed the heresy of the Gnostic Marcion. Inspired by the ideas of St. Justin expressed in the "Dialogo con Trifone". Pius established norms for welcoming the Jews converted to the Christian faith. He us considered to have been particularly rigorous in fighting the relaxation of morals, especially on the part of clerics. During his pontificate St. Justin was beheaded. Tradition states that Pius too was martyred and buried with St. Peter.

11. ANICETUS I, ST. (155-166)

Born in Syria, he came to Rome as a collaborator of St. Justin in the battle against the heretics. He reactivated the decree of St. Anacletus (the third pope) concerning the consecration of bishops and the vestments of the priesthood: no beards or long hair and more rigorously controlled behavior. He confirmed that Easter be celebrated on a Sunday despite the contrary opinion of St. Polycarp who claimed the right to follow his own tradition which came down to him from St. John the Evangelist. In the case of St. Polycarp, Anicetus did not insist or try to dissuade him. Irenaeus recounts that from mutual respect the two did not try to convince each other and "they took their leave in peace". Thus a schism was avoided. Another heresy, Montanism, flourished at that time. Those who professed it claimed to have a more direct divine inspiration. Among the practices of this heresy was a kind of spiritual asceticism accompanied by hysterical frenzies and anti-state attitudes that contributed to throwing a bad light on the Christians from the standpoint of the imperial power. This caused arrests, trials and some convictions. Many were those who were martyred, Polycarp and Anicetus himself among them.

12. SOTER, ST. (166-175)

He was born at Fondi (Latium), but his father was of Greek origin. He fought against various heresies, Montanism, Nicolaism, Adamism and Gnosticism. During this period a violent persecution of the Christians raged at Corinth. St. Soter sent material aid and the comfort of the faith. His generous and charitable action was praised in a letter of thanks sent by Dionysus, bishop of Corinth, to the Roman community. In favor of the Christians, the authoritative voice of the Athenian philosopher Athenagoras was raised who wrote to the Emperor Marcus Aurelius and then to Commodus to ask that the persecutions be stopped. Soter was the first to recognize the sacramental character of marriage. Any union which had not been blessed by a priest was not considered valid. During religious functions he forbade women to burn incense and to touch the Patten and the chalice. This excessively strict attitude towards women is to be attributed to the situation created by the so-called *sinisacte*. These were virginal women, even young ones, who lived together with priests in order to help them, but which created many misunderstandings that sometimes ended in scandal. It is not certain if he was martyred and nothing precise is known about his place of burial.

13. ELEUTHERIUS, ST. (175-189)

Born at Nicopolis in Epirus, he was a disciple of Pope Anicetus whom he assisted as a deacon during his pontificate. He sent Fugazius and Damian to England to convert the peoples there on the request of King Lucius. He dispensed with the obligations of Christians to follow several dietary laws of Judaic origin. During his pontificate there was a continuation of the persecutions unleashed by Marcus Aurelius who was annoyed by the anti-state attitudes of the Montanist sect with whom Christians were confused. To emphasize their total non-involvement in this the Christians had to send the emperor no less than four apologies. St. Cecilia was an illustrious victim of that period. She was found guilty of converting her betrothed Valerian to Christianity. Under Commodus, the son of Marcus Aurelius, there followed a period of relative peace for the Christians. Eleutherius died a martyr.

14. VICTOR I, ST. (189-199)

An African, his papacy coincided with a serene and favorable period for Christianity, thanks to the influence and protection of two women: Marcia and Julia Domna, the wives of Commodus and Septimus Severus respectively. Thus his activities could be directed towards the solution of several important problems. He called a council in 198 to oppose several heresies which were gaining ground. This council was a good occasion to confront and resolve questions of a religious and disciplinary nature. Victor tended not to advise other churches but to impose Rome's ideas on them, thus arousing resentment at times in bishops not inclined to accept such impositions. This was the case of Polycratus, the bishop of Ephesus, who felt offended at this interference. The question was again that of Easter. Victor reaffirmed the decisions of Soter and Eleutherius both with regard to the date, which had to be a Sunday, and with regard to several customs of Jewish origin which were still practised in some Christian communities. An example would be the eating of the pascal lamb at meals. To eliminate several of these customs and to unify the rites in all the churches, Victor charged Polycratus with calling a council. The council concluded that it was licit for everyone to follow their own rites and customs. Polycratus justified himself before the pope with a letter containing the phrase "...it is more important to obey God than men". In time all the Churches conformed.

15. ZEPHYRINUS, ST. (199-217)

He was a Roman and one of his first acts as pope was to make Callistus his secretary and give him the responsibility for administering goods to the community. In particular he was asked to reorganize the cemetery which bears his name. That is the period in which the usage first appeared of putting haloes around the heads of angels, saints and the Blessed Virgin in depicting them. This symbol had already been used in ancient times as an honorific. Zephyrinus pronounced in favor of indissoluble matrimony and defended the rite of baptism against some attempts at perverting it. Zephyrinus was a man of great virtue, but not exceptionally learned or cultured so that he was criticized by the subtle Christian theologian Hyppolitus for being ignorant and not determined enough in fighting the Monarchian heresy. It was a matter of the formula for the Trinity - that is, if the Father and the Son were the same Person and consequently if He had been made flesh. Zephyrinus was martyred under Septimus Severus. Today his remains rest in the Roman Church of San Silvestro in capite.

16. CALLISTUS, ST. (217-222)

He was born in Rome, a scion of the noble Domizii family. After a tumultuous and certainly not edifying life which saw him imprisoned and exiled for common crimes, Callistus finally changed his ways to the point of being chosen by Pope Zephyrinus as his private secretary. At Callistus's election another pope, Hyppolitus, was also elected with the support of some bishops and presbyters, who thus became the first anti-pope in history. There was some violent dissent against Callistus regarding ecclesiastical discipline. Hyppolitus accused Callistus of being too soft. Of himself, he said he was the successor of the apostles and partook equally of the grace of the supreme priesthood. The community he founded lasted for the reigns of three popes: Callistus, Urban and Ponziani. Exiled to Sardinia together with the Pope St. Ponziani, he died in 235. Before his death he became reconciled with the Church which admitted him among its saints. Callistus built and organized the catacombs that are named for him where 46 popes and more than 170,000 martyrs are buried. To him we owe as well the construction of the Basilica of Santa Maria in Trastevere with its many mosaics and the first church dedicated to the Blessed Virgin Mary. Callistus died a martyr's death during an anti-Christian riot and was buried in the cemetery of Caledopius in Via Aurelia.

17. URBAN I, ST. (222-230)

Nothing certain is known of him. He may have been born in Rome and was pope during the reign of Emperor Alexander Severus in a relatively peaceful period for the Christians under the protection of Julia Mamea, the emperor's mother who appears to have been a Christian. He is responsible for the conversion of St. Cecilia, her husband Valentian and her brothers-in-law Maximus and Tiburtius. Urban consented to the acquisition of real estate in the name of the Church. He was decapitated by the police chief Turcius Almenius, and his body, salvaged by Julia Mamea, was buried in the catacombs of St. Callistus. Today it rests in the Roman Church of San Prassede while a part of his relics ended up in France.

18. PONTIAN, ST. (230-235)

He was born in Rome. During his papacy the Church was subjected to some persecution from the Emperors Alexander Severus and Maximinus Thrax. Pontian himself was one of the victims, deported to Sardinia and subjected to a very hard life. It seems that before dying he renounced the papacy in order that the Church give itself a new pastor who would be present in Rome. But this information is uncertain. He died of exhaustion and suffering, for which reason the Church numbers him among the saints. His remains rest in the Roman Church of San Prassede. He confirmed the condemnation by Demetrius of Alexandria of several of Origen's writings which led directly to the Gnostic heresy. He ordered that the psalms be sung in churches, prescribed the recitation of the *Confiteor* before the mass and recommended that it be recited to the dying as well. The formulation *Dominus vobiscum* has been authoritatively traced back to his times.

19. ANTERUS, ST. (235-236)

A Greek from Magna Grecia, he took care that all the records of Christian martyrs be collected and preserved in the churches. He also began an official record of the acts of the Church which were kept in a place called a *scrinium*. This collection was burned under Diocletian. It was begun again and this time disappeared again during the time of Honorius III (1225). He was pope for only a few months while Pontian was still alive and he was martyred under Maximinus. His body was transferred to the papal crypt in the Catacombs of San Callisto. Today his relics are conserved in the Church of San Silvestro in capite.

20. FABIAN, ST. (236-250)

He was born in Rome. There was no consensus on whom to elect after Anterus, and it is related that during the heat of the discussion a dove settled on the head of Fabian who was passing there by chance. This was interpreted as being a sign from God and Fabian was elected at once. He turned out to be an excellent administrator and immediately dedicated himself to organizing the Roman dioceses, completing, in effect, the project of Pope Evaristus. He divided the city into seven sections, each of which with a deacon at its head who job was to organize charity and manage the distribution of alms to the needy. Under the Emperor Decius there was such a ferocious persecution that many Christians were induced to flee Rome and the big cities to find refuge in the deserts of Arabia and the Thebaid as well as to lead solitary lives of repentance. These hermits or anchorites were famous for saintliness and small groups of disciples formed around them. These were the origins of the first ancient monasteries (Paul the Hermit, Hilary, Pachomius...). Unlike these saints, many Christians abandoned the faith from fear of being killed: this was the sad phenomenon of the *lapsi* ("the lapsed"), the fallen, the apostates. Fabian did not leave Rome and was martyred there. His remains are conserved today in the Roman Church of San Prassede.

21. CORNELIUS, ST. (251-253)

Born in Rome, his election followed upon harsh battles. He was opposed by the priest Novatian who proclaimed himself pope with support from Carthage. The two of them maintained a severe puritanism in respect to the so-called *lapsi* - the Christians who had abandoned the faith - and who, according to them, ought not to be re-admitted into the bosom of the Church. Thus they accused Cyprian and Cornelius of weakness and lack of determination. Cornelius called a council that condemned Novatian, calling him an anti-pope. Under Cornelius's pontificate Origen died who was bishop of Alexandria and a doctor of the Greek Church. Origen had expressed some heterodox ideas but had fought hard against the pagan philosopher Celsus who had written against Christianity. The Emperor Trebonianus Gallus accused Cornelius of having offended the pagan gods, thus provoking a contagious disease that had struck Rome and part of the empire. Therefore he was ordered to make sacrifices to the gods, and on refusing he was exiled to Civitavecchia where he died in 253. He was not a martyr, but the Church considers him such. He was buried in the church of Santa Maria in Trastevere in Rome.

22. LUCIUS I, ST. (253-254)

Born in Rome, as soon as he was elected he was exiled to an unknown place but was allowed to return to Rome thanks to the benevolence of the Emperor Valerian. In his brief papacy he fought against the loosening of morals which many prelates had fallen into. Cohabitation between deaconesses and clerics was becoming more and more customary for the purposes of charity and assistance. And lapses were becoming just as frequent. Lucius prohibited such cohabitation and extended to laymen the ban on living with women outside marriage unless they were very close relatives. He also prescribed that in his movements the pope be accompanied by three deacons and at least two priests. Lucius died from natural causes and was buried in the papal crypt of the San Callisto Cemetery. Today he rests in the Roman church of St. Cecilia.

23. STEPHEN I, ST. (254-257)

He was a Roman noble at the head of one of the seven diaconates. He was bishop of Rome during a tranquil period under the Emperor Valerian. Therefore he was able to dedicate himself to the internal affairs of the Church. The most burning question was the primacy of the Roman Church above all the others, and it was a thorny one. In fact, he came into conflict with Cyprian, the bishop of Carthage, and with many of the other African and Asian churches. They did not want to accept his dictates regarding the baptizing of heretics or dissidents who wanted to return to the bosom of the Church. Cyprian maintained that heresy cancelled baptism and so those who after erring wanted to return to the Church would have to be rebaptized. For his part, Stephen, more traditionally, insisted that no new baptism was needed and that it would be enough to impose a penance on the heretics. The question was resolved many years later when both Stephen and Cyprian were dead. The Roman view prevailed. In 257 Valerian unleashed a great persecution on the Christians, accusing them of wanting to take over state property. Bishops, priests and deacons were the main targets and many of them were killed. Stephen too was probably martyred and was buried in the papal crypt of San Callisto.

24. SIXTUS II, ST. (257-258)

Born in Athens, he was a man of great culture and doctrine. He was called "the peace lover" and, in fact, he hurried to bring a modicum of peace to the relations between the Roman and Carthaginian Churches which were in harsh opposition over the question of rebaptizing heretics. (See St. Stephen. no. 23) He brought about a reconciliation with St. Cyprian, but before he could pursue the dialog further he had to face a new emergency: the Emperor Valerian unleashed a second persecution of Christians. They were made to abjure or face confiscation of their property and beheading. Sixtus was arrested, tried and condemned. History tells of a moving encounter with his deacon, St. Lawrence, while he was being conducted to his death. St. Lawrence asked to be allowed to die with him, but Sixtus replied lovingly with the prediction that St. Lawrence would soon suffer a more glorious death in the name of Christ. And in fact, four days later, was to die by burning alive on a grill. In that same encounter he asked St. Lawrence to distribute the treasures of the Church to the poor. Sixtus was conducted to the catacombs of San Pretestato and was beheaded while seated on his episcopal chair. He was buried in the papal crypt of San Callisto.

25. DIONYSIUS, ST. (259-268)

His origins are unknown. He was elected after a year with the papal seat vacant because of Valerian's persecutions. Dionysius was a simple priest. Thanks to the freedom and tranquillity the Christians enjoyed under the new Emperor Gallienus, son of Valerian, Dionysius was able to devote himself to the internal affairs of the Church. The writings of Tertullian, Cyprian, and other Christian apologists and philosophers circulated freely. This not only favored Christianity's penetrating of the Roman world, but allowed for a more attentive and precise working out of the doctrine itself. Under these circumstances, Dionysius reorganized the Church of Rome, giving it back the position of supremacy it had enjoyed before the polemics of St. Cyprian. In this sense, many profited from the substantial aid that the pope sent to the disaster-struck Eastern churches which were in still greater difficulty because of the barbarian invasions. He ransomed many Christian prisoners and had many destroyed churches rebuilt. On the level of doctrine, he opposed the Monarchianist heresy that Sabellius had dusted off... He reduced the concept of the Trinity to a question of words while, in effect, he stated that it was "one person". This doctrine was condemned in a council held in 265. Another theologian of the Trinity, the Bishop Paul of Samothrace, was making proselytes at Antioch in those days. He wa connected to Queen Zenobia who had given him power over the city and, in return for the favor, he worked out a Trinity doctrine based on some of her ideas. According to this theory, Christ had become God "progressively and by adoption". After various vicissitudes during three councils, the theory was condemned and Paul excommunicated, deposed and exiled. Dionysius died in 268 and was buried in the papal crypt of the Catacombs of San Callisto.

26. FELIX I, ST. (269-274)

Born in Rome, he was pope under the Emperor Aurelian in a period which began quite serenely. A letter is attributed to him which was addressed to Maximus, bishop of Alexandria, concerning the Most Holy Trinity, a subject then much under discussion. This letter was considered of great importance at the Council of Ephesus in 431. The text while synthetic is very precise and reads thus: <<Our faith in the Incarnation is that which comes down from the Apostles. We believe that the Lord Jesus Christ, born of the Blessed Virgin Mary, is the Word, the eternal Son of God and not a man different from God whom God Himself raised to this honor. The Son of God did not choose a man to associate with Himself; two persons do not exist in Christ. The Word, God most perfect, was incarnated in the womb of the Blessed Virgin and became perfect man>>. Felix deposed the Bishop of Antioch, Paul of Samothrace, after his doctrine was condemned as erroneous in this matter. He also fought against Manicheism which negated the essence of Christ, admitting only two principles that govern the world, good and evil. Felix I died a martyr and was buried in the Roman Church of San Prassede.

27. EUTYCHIAN, ST. (275-283)

He was born at Luni in Etruria. Very little is known about him. It is known that his pontificate was under the reign of the Emperor Probus when the Church was much persecuted and the martyrs many. He ordered them to receive great honors. More than 300 he buried himself. He did not want them buried in simple white shrouds, as was normal, but in red Dalmatics, rich tunics reserved for the emperor. In today's liturgy they are worn by deacons during the solemn functions. He died a martyr and was buried in the Cemetery of San Callisto.

28. GAIUS or CAIUS, St. (283-296)

Born in Dalmatia, he was a nephew of the Emperor Diocletian. Diocletian was the one to order the bloodiest of all persecutions of the Christians, perhaps because he understood the revolutionary potential of the new religion and its potential to disrupt the absolute power of the state. In his eyes, then, the persecution would have been an obligatory act in defence of Roman society against Christianity which attacked its basic principles. It was a battle for survival. Gaius concerned himself with reorganizing the ecclesiastical hierarchy, establishing that only those who had already been ordained on lower levels could be nominated as bishops. He died a martyr, not on order of his uncle but of Maximillian. He is buried in Rome in the Church of San Silvestro in capite.

29. MARCELLINUS ST. (269-304)

Born in Rome, he was pope at the time that Diocletian unleashed the tenth persecution against the Christians. This was total war. There was no sector in which they were not struck: besides being killed, they were excluded from public office, had their property confiscated and were exiled. Churches were destroyed and holy books burned. Many were the illustrious martyrs of that period. Marcellinus was accused by the Donatist heretics of having made sacrifices to the gods to escape death. But the accusation was false. He was martyred on Christmas day 304. His remains are conserved in the Roman Church of the SS. Apostoli.

30. MARCELLUS I, ST. (308-309)

Born in Rome, he was elected about four years after the death of Marcellinus because of the terrible conditions in which the Christians lived under Diocletian's persecutions. During the very short time in which he could fulfil his mandate, he made a few very important decisions: first, he prohibited the convocation of any general council without the authorization of the Roman pope; the second established the procedures to be followed when pardoning Christians who had recanted from fear during the persecutions. Marcellus refused to burn incense to the gods. The new emperor Maxentius had him arrested and condemned him to work in the imperial stables to humiliate him. Freed by Christians, he took refuge in the home of the matron Lucina who allowed him to convert her house into a church. When this was discovered he was arrested again and this time forced to work as custodian in the very church that the emperor had meanwhile had made into a stable. Marcellus died in privation and humiliation. He was buried in the Cemetery of Priscilla.

31. EUSEBIUS, ST. (309-309)

He was probably born in Magna Grecia and was pope for only four months. He too had to come to grips with the question of pardoning the apostates who wanted to return to the Church. Since the question was most delicate caution was necessary and the application of clear and rigorous norms valid for everyone. Errors of evaluation and an easy-going handling could have provoked discontent and doubt as well as fomenting polemics with negative consequences for the whole Christian community. Eusebius died a martyr under the Emperor Maxentius and was buried at San Callisto. His remains were later transferred to San Sebastiano fuori le mura.

32. MILTIADES or MELCHIADES, ST. (311-314)

Born in Africa, his name is bound to the most important historical-political event in Christianity of those times: the Edict of Constantine promulgated in Milan in 313, thanks to which the Christian religion could be freely practised along with all the other religions of the Empire without fear of persecution. The freedom sanctioned by law together with other aid furnished by the imperial authorities created an extreme expansion of Christianity so as to reverse its previous proportions with regard to the pagan religion. It soon became the state religion and entered quite justifiably onto the world scene and into history. Undoubtedly the influence of his mother St. Helen and sister St. Constance, already Christians, that contributed to Constantine's the decision to make the edict. But there was an even weightier reason of a political nature: by now there were simply too many Christians in all sectors of social and political life from the lowest to the highest. Constantine gave Miltiades a grotto in the Lateran Palace which was turned into a baptistery. Alongside it he had built the Basilica of San Giovanni in Laterano. Miltiades died in 314. He is buried in the Roman Church of San Silvestro in capite.

33. SILVESTER I, ST. (314-335)

Born in Rome, he governed the Church for many years in the new climate of freedom that Constantine had created. The emperor gave Silvester the Lateran Palace as his seat. The palace was called Patriarchio. He concerned himself not only with the building of churches (the basilicas of St. John, St. Peter and St. Paul) but also defended the faith against the attacks of numerous heretical doctrines which began to spring up everywhere, encouraged by peace and freedom. The most extensive and damaging of them was the Arian heresy which, in effect, denied the Trinity. Thus he called a council, the first ecumenical one, at Nicaea in Asia Minor, at which, in the presence of the Emperor Constantine, the Arian teaching was condemned and the divinity of Christ and his consubstantiality with the Father was reaffirmed. The *Credo* was composed which is the compendium of all the truths of the Christian faith. Silvester baptized Constantine in Jerusalem on the occasion of the consecration of the Church of the Holy Sepulchre on the Calvary at the behest of St. Helen. Sunday was instituted as the Day of the Lord and he appears to have been the first one to wear the tiara from which the bishop's mitre is derived. He died on December 31 and was buried in the Roman church which bears his name.

34. MARK, ST. (336-336)

Born in Rome, he was pope for only a few months. The struggle against the Arian heresy, aided by other emminent clerics - Athanasius, Hilary, Basil - absorbed all his energy. In his own way even Constantine lent a hand acting on his own without giving a thought to Mark, just as he had never given a thought to Silvester. It is enough just to look at how he behaved in the business between Arius and Bishop Athanasius, readmitting Arius into the Church of Alexandria and exiling Athanasius to Trier without consulting or even informing the pope. At that time the first Church calender was drawn up. A decree is attributed to Mark which reserves the right of consecrating the pope to the bishop of Ostia. He seems to be the first to have used the Pallium, a kind of white band with black fringes, worn by the pope, the patriarchs and metropolitans who hang it around their necks over the holy vestments. The wool of two white lambs is used to make it. Palliums which have been blessed are conserved in a silver casket near the tomb of St. Peter. He had the Church of San Marco Evangelista constructed in Rome and was later buried there.

35. JULIUS I, ST. (337-352)

He was born in Rome. At the point of death Constantine expressed the wish to recall Athanasius, bishop of Alexandria, whom he had exiled, and have him put back in his bishop's see. Constantine's son Constantius initially agreed, then opposed the idea and even had Athanasius exiled again. Athanasius appealed to Pope Julius who called a council in Rome which completely rehabilitated Athanasius. But he could not return to Alexandria because of the open hostility of the Arians with whom Constantius sympathized and because of the presence of the new Bishop Gregory of Capodacia whom the emperor had imposed. Another council had to be called and, by agreement with Julius, Constantius convened it at Serdica, today Sofia, which again completely rehabilitated Athanasius. But to take possession of his seat again, he had to await the death of Gregory who was under Constantius's protection. This council established the canons governing the reform of ecclesiastical discipline in line with the Council of Nicaea. A concept was formulated that would be the basis of the supremacy of the Roman Church in matters of discipline, law and faith: it established that any decisions made by councils or individual bishoprics had to be ratified by Rome before becoming definitive. Julius himself had previously written to the Eastern bishops in these words: "Whenever questions arise, one must first of all write to us, according to the custom, so that here, in justice, the question may be resolved". These continual expressions of position were made necessary by the repeated attempts on the part of the imperial power to take command in matters that were often entirely religious. To this pope is owed the establishment of the archives of the Holy See. He also ordered that the Eastern Church celebrate Christmas on December 25 and not on January 6 as it had done until then. His remains are conserved in the Roman Church of Santa Maria in Trastevere.

36. LIBERIUS (352-366)

Born in Rome to the Savelli family, his pontificate was marked by controversies arising from the interference of the Emperor Constantius who openly championed the Arian heresy and the attempt of Julian the Apostate to reestablish the old pagan cult. Immediately solicited by the Arians to disavow Athanasius, the bishop of Alexandria, he convened a council in Rome which vindicated Athanasius. The Arians, in effect, were trying to strike at the symbol of the Nicaean council. It was then that Liberius decided a new council was required to look into the matter more deeply. He made a request on this basis to the Emperor Constantius who first held a council at Arles imposing on the fathers who attended the condemnation of Athanasius and the papal legates. Liberius deplored the behavior of the bishops and would not accept the decisions. He demanded another council which was held in Milan and where Constantius, more determined than ever, repeated his performance, extorting the assent of the bishops with threats of exile. Athanasius was again condemned and the Nicaean Creed repudiated. Liberius indignantly refused to give his assent and was exiled to France. But the Roman populace demanded the return of the pope and Constantius saw himself forced to recall Liberius. But he imposed two heavy conditions: that he agree to share the papacy with Felix, the anti-pope whom Constantius had elected, and the signing of a document that contained a formulation very close to the Arian thesis. The first condition was spared him by the Roman people who loved him and chased Felix out of Rome. With regard to the second, however, he was criticized by many (Athanasius, Hilary of Poitiers, Jerome) who saw this submission as a weakness due to the fear of death. With the death of Constantius there was an end to the nightmare of the Arian heresy. But his successor, Julian the Apostate created a new danger, determined, as he was, to reestablish the pagan religion. Pope Liberius had the Church of Santa Maria Maggiore built on the Esquiline hill on the spot where legend says a miraculous snow fall occurred on the night of August 3-4. Liberius is buried in the Vatican grottoes.

37. DAMASUS I, ST. (366-384)

Born in Spain to a family of the nobility, another pope, Ursinus, was almost immediately elected by a restricted number of priests and deacons to oppose him. Damasus was forced to fight him, even with armed force, to defend his own election. After changing vicissitudes, during which Damasus was the object of accusations and calumnies, Ursinus was finally exiled by the Emperor Gratian and the legitimate pope could dedicate himself to restoring lustre and authority to the papacy. He succeeded in imposing the supremacy of Rome over the other churches so that he was finally accepted universally. St. Ambrose, the bishop of Milan, himself stated in an extremely concise formulation: "Where Peter is, there is the Church". Two councils had made laws to that effect, the one in Rome in 369, and the one in Antioch in 378. But Damasus went further by affirming that Rome was supreme not because any council had so decided, but because Jesus had put Peter above all others, making him the corner-stone of the entire Church. He lavished attention on evangelizing and Christianizing all of Roman society on all levels, helped in this by St. Jerome the great preacher and crowd hypnotizer whom he chose as his secretary. Other valid help came from the emperors Gratian and Theodosius who openly supported the Church of Rome. Damasus can be considered the first of the great papal patrons in history by commissioning the big revision of the Gospels in Latin from St. Jerome which contributed largely to making the whole Christian message more compact. He undertook the construction of various churches and the restoration of the catacombs giving a strong impetus to the cult of the martyrs. He was buried in the Church of San Lorenzo in Damaso which had been built by him.

38. SIRICIUS, ST. (384-399)

Born in Rome, he was a deacon under popes Liberius and Damasus. Elected by acclamation, he was the first to assume the title of pope from the Greek *papa* meaning father. He enjoyed the esteem and friendship of the Emperor Valentinian II, but not that of St. Jerome who in any case had no liking for any of the Roman clergy. He followed Damasus' rigorous and "monarchist" line, reaffirming the supremacy of the bishop of Rome and claiming authority over the most important decisions regarding ecclesiastical discipline and law. His writings are like imperial decrees where a statement is not based on legality but is its own justification. Siricius neither exhorts nor admonishes as his predecessors did; he simply commands and prohibits. He held a synod in Rome where the primacy of the Church of Rome over all the others was affirmed. Celibacy was prescribed for priests and deacons and it was decreed that only bishops could ordain priests and that monks too could become bishops. St. Augustine's conversion took place at that time. He was an energetic man capable of commanding respect on all occasions. The Emperor Theodosius, for example, had sinned very gravely by destroying the rebellious city of Thessalonica and killing over 7,000 people. Repentant, he asked to be readmitted to the bosom of the Church. Pope Siricius pardoned him, but demanded he make amends and humiliate himself publicly. Another example of his severity and authority was when he condemned the monk Jovinian and expelled him from the Church because after a life of fasting and self-mortification he had come to preach the complete equality between purity and carnal sin. A Christian, he said, once he has "deeply assimilated the meaning of baptism", can no longer sin. This doctrine gave free rein to any kind of dissolute behavior. It was harshly opposed by St. Jerome and St. Ambrose. Siricius is buried in the Church of San Prassede in Rome.

39. ANASTASIUS I, ST. (399-401)

He was born to the Massimi family in Rome and was elected pope just a day after the death of Siricius. He banned the works of Origen whose ideas were considered heretical. He established several religious rites, prescribing that priests must listen to the reading of the Gospels with bare and bowed heads. Another of his rules was that no one with an invalidating physical defect could become a priest. He was buried in the Ursum Pileatum cemetery in Via Portuense. Today his remains rest in the church of San Martino ai Monti in Rome.

40. INNOCENT I, ST. (401-417)

Born in Albano outside Rome, St. Jerome says he was the son of Anastasius I. His was a strong personality as testify his decretals on discipline. He personally experienced the full force of the invasion by Alaric and his Goths, taking part in the Roman delegation to Honorius, holed-up at Ravenna, but unable to convince him to move against Alaric. By now Alaric was at the gates of Rome. The first time he lifted his siege in exchange for a large amount of money, but the next year he returned and sacked the city ferociously (410). Using the full weight of his authority, Innocent convinced Alaric, who was a Christian, even if an Arian, to spare many human lives and to respect the churches, in particular the basilicas of the apostles Peter and Paul where many citizens had taken refuge. He defended John Chrysostom, archbishop of Constaninople, against the attacks of the Empress Eudoxia, who was irritated by his intransigence towards the vanity of women and of Eudoxia in particular. Eudoxia had John exiled twice despite the repeated intervention of Innocent. Another great battle completely absorbed his attention: that against the Manichaean heresy and the English monk Pelagius. The Pelagian heresy gave importance only to free will for salvation and not at all to divine grace. Nor did it admit of original sin. He got the Emperor Honorius to make a severe law against heretics and to enforce the old edict of Constantine prohibiting circus spectacles. He was buried near his father Anastasius.

41. ZOSIMUS, ST. (417-418)

A Greek, he was elected on the suggestion of Pope Innocent. His pontificate was brief and troubled by the Pelagian heresy that continued to spread. He was ingenuous, however, because he rehabilitated Caelestius the Pelagian who had been condemned by St. Augustine and the African bishops at the Council of Carthage. He persisted in his position until a new council repeated the same condemnation. At this point Zosimus, in a letter entitled *Tractoria*, condemned Pelagianism and defined the dogma of original sin, indicating divine grace as the only means of spiritual salvation. He made another wrong move when he ruled that priests and deacons who had been excommunicated by African bishops could appeal to Rome or nearby Churches for judgement and rehabilitation. This disposition was seen as an undue incursion into disciplinary matters. But there were no aftereffects thanks to the conciliatory attitude of the African bishops who did not make problems. He ruled that illegitimate children and slaves could not become clerics. His remains are conserved in the Roman Church of San Lorenzo fuori le mura.

42. BONIFACE I, ST. (418-422)

He was born in Rome. Immediately after the death of Zosimus a part of the populace elected the arch-deacon Eulalius as pope while the majority of the clergy and the rest of the people elected an old priest, Boniface. The two factions could not come to terms and the decision was put into the hands of the Emperor Honorius. He ordered the two contenders to keep away from Rome while a council made the decision. Boniface was confirmed. Honorius established that for the future, when there were two contenders, only the one who received a unanimous vote could be elected pope. The Pelagian heresy was the source of problems for Boniface who maintained the condemnation made by Innocent and Zosimus. He repeated, almost identically, the error made by Zosimus with regard to the African Church and to St. Augustine by allowing the reintegration of a certain Bishop Antony who had been deposed as unworthy by St. Augustine. This caused a certain tension between the two Churches, but there were no repercussions.

43. CELESTINE I, ST. (422-432)

Born in Campania, he was a friend of St. Augustine, and this facilitated the reconciliation with the African Church (see the preceding pope). Rome kept its primacy, but the African Church was autonomous in disciplinary matters. In these years the terrible Vandal invasion of North Africa took place which put the Church there into its death agonies. Under his pontificate the problem brought up by Nestorius was solved who affirmed that the Blessed Virgin should be called "the Mother of Christ" and not "the Mother of God". Celestine was asked to intervene and he condemned Nestorius. But the Emperor Theodosius II, who favored Nestorius, wanted a council to decide the matter. Thus an ecumenical council was convened at Ephesus which upheld Nestorius's condemnation. Theodosius accepted the decision and Nestorius retired to a monastery in Egypt where he died. Celestine spurred the missions to Scotland and Ireland through the work of Palladius and St. Patrick. In his writings the first use is made of the word *pastoral*, as a token of the bishops' pastoral jurisdiction. The pope uses it too, but only as the bishop of Rome. He was buried in the cemetery of Priscilla.

44. SIXTUS III, ST. (432-440)

Born in Rome, like Celestine he condemned the doctrines of Pelagius and Nestorius and rejected the appeal of Eutherius who had come to Rome to defend the latter's cause. The last summits on the question were held and the Madonna was universally recognized as "the Mother of God". To commemorate the event, Sixtus had the Church of Santa Maria Maggiore built. He had it adorned with exceptionally luxurious furnishings and decorations including the splendid mosaics which are still to be seen along the walls of the central nave, above the trabeation and in the triumphal arch. Sixtus constructed and had restored many other churches and holy places in Rome, including Constantine's Lateran Baptistery and San Lorenzo in Lucina. He was buried in San Lorenzo fuori le mura.

45. LEO I, ST. (440-461)

Born in Volterra in Etruria, he was elected unanimously by the clerics and the people. With him the papacy assumed the distinguishing characteristic of absolute and unquestioned authority in matters of discipline and the defence of the faith. For this reason he is generally considered "the first pope". Not only did he exceed all his predecessors in attributing this role to himself, but he was an example for succeeding generations, the ideal figure of the pope of Rome. He expended the same courage and commitment in facing the two main problems of his time: heretics and barbarians. Among the heresies he fought was the one preached by the Greek Eutyches who had the Emperor Theodosius II on his side. Eutychianism was the opposite of Arianism in that it emphasized the divine nature of Christ to the point of obliterating His human side. Leo demanded that a council be called to definitively decide the serious problem. That was only possible after the death of Theodosius. He called it in Chalcedon and two fundamental decisions were made there: a dogmatic decree was emanated on the incarnation inspired by the doctrine of council of Nicaea and the acceptance of Leo's teachings extending over the bishop of Constantinople, Flavian. After hearing Leo's letter, the assembly commented: "Peter has spoken through the mouth of Leo". It was the recognition of Rome's primacy. The affair of Attila, king of the Huns, brought Leo unconditional authority. The former was ready to occupy Rome, but he hesitated. Then an embassy was sent to him which included Pope Leo who was Attila's principle counterpart in the discussions. It is not known exactly what Leo told the great barbarian, but the fact remains that he retreated. Leo certainly used arguments of an economic and political nature rather than spiritual ideas or threats. But many legends grew up around the pope and this event. He did not have the same success in dealing with the Vandal Gaiseric who, due to an intrigue fomented at the court of the Empress Eudossia invaded Rome and sacked it savagely. Gaiseric only promised him to spare the basilicas of St. Peter, St. Paul, and St. John Lateran. Nothing else was spared. It was June 455 and there were two weeks of terror, destruction and despoiling. The Vandals took away thousands of citizens as slaves, among them Eudossia herself who had been the cause of so many ills. There was nothing for Leo to do but reconstruct his beloved city reduced to a rubble heap. Many of his letters and sermons survive. He was buried in the old St. Peter's Basilica.

46. HILARUS, ST. (461-468)

He was born at Cagliari in Sardinia. He had already distinguished himself as one of Leo's papal legates to the council of Ephesus. Not many of his documents remain, but it is certain that he was trained in Leo's high school. He showed firmness in confronting the Emperor Anthemius who was protecting a community of heretics headed by a certain Philoteus. He concerned himself with the education of the clergy and ordered that neither popes nor bishops could choose their successors. At the Lateran he established two libraries that provided the first nucleus of the Vatican one. He took great interest in the adornment of oratories and monasteries, not sparing expense and making lavish use of gold, silver and other precious materials. He loved rich display and in that he was not a good disciple of Leo who was also attentive to the problems of the people. It was a time of great poverty with which this rich ostentation on the part of the Church clashed stridently. He is buried in San Lorenzo fuori le mura.

47. SIMPLICIUS, ST. (468-483)

Born in Tivoli, during his reign the Western Empire came to an end under the blows of the barbarians in whose hands Italy remained. The first barbarian king was Odoacre. He was of the Arian faith but allowed freedom of religious practice. The new political situation had led to the rupture between Italy and Constantinople thus making Rome a distant provincial capital. The voice of the pope had less resonance and authority just as his person was less influential in the exchange between East and West. But for the same reason his importance and influence grew in the West. From this time on, the pope and the Church of Rome become the cardinal point around which turn all the politics and life of the West until modern times. Simplicius dedicated himself to organizing the patrimony of the Holy See and he turned out to be an excellent administrator. He continued the construction work of Hilarius. But Simplicius's major concern was not the barbarians who showed themselves, all told, to be worthy successors to the empire. Rather it was the old and new heresies that occupied him. He sent priests everywhere to fight against the Arian heresy and the Eutychian one which was even professed by the Eastern Emperor Zeno.

48. FELIX III, ST. (483-492)

He was born in Rome to the noble Anicia family and was elected on the suggestion of Odoacre. He tried to raise the Rome Church to the levels it had enjoyed under Pope Leo. For this reason he sent two bishops to Constantinople to ask for explanations concerning the behavior of the Patriarch Acacius who, with the support of the Emperor Zeno, had deposed the bishop of Alexandria. Acacius bought off the two bishops who did not conclude their assignment and were thus removed and excommunicated by Felix. Acacius was also excommunicated for ignoring the word of the Roman pontiff and thus creating the first schism which lasted 35 years. But Felix took a more benevolent approach towards Zeno that was, all told, marked by paternal understanding. He limited himself to advising him to follow the will of the legitimate bishops if he wanted to save himself and not go against the divine will. He is the first pope to address the emperor with the word "my son". Zeno did not follow his advice but rather indicated his annoyance at such interference and familiarity. He went so far as to push Theodoric, king of the Ostrogoths, to move against Odoacre, the friend and protector of Felix. The manuever succeeded: Theodoric took his place as king of Italy, but by then both Felix and Zeno were dead. Felix was the only pope to be buried in the Basilica of San Paolo fuori le mura.

49. GELASIUS I, ST. (492-496)

Born in Africa, he was secretary of Felix III. He tried to reach a conciliation between the Eastern and Western Churches as his predecessor had already tried to do. He did not succeed, partly because of the scoffing opposition of the Emperor Anastasius. Still famous is the letter Gelasius wrote to this emperor to clarify his ideas about the two powers, temporal and spiritual. Of the two, the spiritual is higher and even the emperor must bow to it. The latter is limited to the exercise of temporal power. For their part, even the ministers of God must submit to the imperial laws in material matters. And if it is right that the faithful are under the tutelage of the bishops, it is just as necessary that all acknowledge the supremacy of the head of that Church which God had established as being above all others, which is to say, the Church of Rome. Never had a discourse been more clear. He worked to cancel out the last residues of the pagan rites and festivals which still persisted in the habits of the Christians. He did not hesitate to make use of the riches of the Church to help meet the needs of the people in times of famine, pestilence or simple poverty. He was called "the pope of the poor people."

50. ANASTASIUS II, ST. (496-498)

Born in Rome, he was a weak and excessively conciliatory character. Wanting to put an end to the schism he showed himself willing to make concessions to the Eastern Church that proposed the monophysite position of Eutyches. In so doing he created much ill will towards himself from both the clergy and the populace. He was not up to the level of Gelasius, especially not in keeping up the prestige and authority of the Roman Church. He himself was accused of heresy and went down in history with this reputation so that he was even consigned by Dante to hell. During his pontificate, Clovis, the king of the Franks, converted to Christianity.

51. SYMMACHUS, ST. (498-514)

He was born in Sardinia. On the very day of his election another faction elected the archpriest Lawrence in opposition to him. But Theodoric, asked to intervene, decreed that Symmachus had been legitimately elected. Lawrence would not give in and used every means, not excluding calumny, to defend his own election. The controversy was resolved by a council of 125 bishops which confirmed Symmachus. The story of this election, the accusations and the calumnies of his opposers occupied his time and made his life difficult for many years. He opposed and excommunicated the Emperor Anastasius because he supported Acacius and because he had treated him arrogantly and even injuriously. He took care to beautify Rome with new churches and buildings. Attributed to him is the first nucleus of what was to become the Vatican Palace where the popes went to live after the return from Avignon. he declared the possession of ecclesiastical property to be legitimate and gave the clergy the use of such.

52. HORMISDAS, ST. (514-523)

Born at Frosinone, it was during his pontificate that the definitive reconciliation took place between the Eastern and Western Churches. He showed ability and authority in negotiating. At Constantinople the so-called "Hormisdas formula" was signed that reproposed essentially the doctrine of the councils of Nicaea, Chalcedon, and the letter of Pope Leo the Great. It ended with the words: "...I agree with the doctrine professed by the pope and reprove all those who reprove him". In politics, on the other hand, there was a distinct fracture between East and West due to the Emperor Justin. The latter wanted reconquer Italy and join it to the empire. But he had to take Theodoric into account. Against him, an Arian, he used the weapon of religion counting on the support of the pope and the Catholics. Thus he roused the Italian people against him and by an edict began the persecution of the Arians going so far as to close their church. Theodoric retaliated by persecuting the Catholics whom he held responsible for the emperor's policy. Hormisdas made laws regarding ecclesiastical discipline: bishops must not be ordained in exchange for privileges and donations. It was during his pontificate that St. Benedict founded his order.

53. JOHN I, ST. (523-526)

Born in Tuscany, his was a brief pontificate and very stormy. He had to undergo all the damages ensuing from Theodoric's hostility and persecutions. The latter was convinced that the Senate and bishop of Rome were at the bottom of Justin's persecution of the Arians. For this reason he had Senator Symmachus and the philosopher Boethius killed for high treason. On the demand of Theodoric, John went to Constantinople to entreat the Emperor Justin to stop the persecution of the Arians. He was the first pope to go to Constantinople. He was greeted triumphantly as the head of Christianity. On that occasion he solemnly crowned the emperor. He obtained the revocation of the edict against the Arians, but did not obtain consent - because he did not even request it - for repentant Arians to return to their faith as Theodoric had expressly demanded. This fact angered the Ostrogoth king who kept the pope a prisoner at Ravenna when he went there to make his report. John died in Ravenna and was only afterwards removed to Rome where he was buried in the Vatican grottoes. An inscription calls him *victima Christi*.

54. FELIX IV, ST. (526-530)

He was possibly born at Benevento. He was certainly a choice imposed by Theodoric, but he was accepted in view of the reigning climate of terror. Theodoric died a few weeks later and thus the persecutions stopped, thanks in part to the good relations between the pope and Amalasuntha, the regent for the child king Athalaric. Felix managed to have the bishop of Rome named judge in controversies between the clergy and the laity and superior to the civil courts. For his part he ordered that no aspiring priests should be ordained who did not show a strong vocation. He was ill. He was so worried that at his death the Church could undergo tensions or schisms over his successor that he called upon a 529 edict of Symmachus's for designating his own successor. He passed the pallium to the archdeacon Boniface who did, in fact, succeed him. In those years the Benedictine order spread throughout Italy and the famous Abbey of Montecassino was built.

55. BONIFACE II (530-532)

He was born in Rome but of German descent. Felix IV had designated him as his successor and a part of the clergy agreed to honor his last will. But a larger group of priests opposed him with an anti-pope, Dioscorus of Alexandria who lived only 22 days after being nominated. With that, Boniface received obedience from his adversaries as well. His one concern seems to have been that of providing himself with a successor. In fact, he made the Roman clergy swear in writing that the same thing would not occur again as happened when he was elected. He imposed the deacon Vigilius as his successor. At this point the Senate intervened accusing the pope of abuse of power and called on him to defend himself before a council. Boniface went, burnt the sworn declaration in front of the assembly and in this way avoided being judged. This probably cost him a place in the official list of saints. In fact, he is the first pope not to be declared a saint. On that occasion rules were established for the election of the pope; in particular it was expressly forbidden to give money or gifts in order to obtain a post or a benefit. It was the last decree emanated by the Roman Senate.

56. JOHN I (533-535)

Mercury, which was his real name, was born in Rome. He asked Athalaric to make a decree against simony "which corrupted the nominations of bishops and influenced negatively the election of the pope himself". Athalaric not only granted him the decree, although reserving for himself the right to ratify the election, but also earmarked a certain sum of money for the expenses that might be incurred in the case of a contested election and for battles which Ravenna might be asked to resolve. But Athalaric died soon afterwards as did Amalasuntha, murdered on a small island in the lake of Bolsena where she had been sent by her husband Theodahad who married her at the last minute to save the kingdom of the Goths. Meanwhile Justin, who was preparing to take back control of Italy, sent John II rich gifts for St. Peter's Basilica and a profession of the orthodox faith which reaffirmed the divine maternity of Mary and the doctrine on the Person of Jesus Christ.

57. AGAPITUS I, ST. (535-536)

Born in Rome to the noble Anicia family and very firm in his faith, he committed himself totally to carrying out his ministry as his many remaining letters testify. As soon as he was elected he found himself facing a difficult problem: Belisarius, Justin's general, had invaded Italy to fight against the Goth Theodahad, with the intention of bringing the peninsula back under the control of Constantinople. The Ostrogothic king charged the pope to intervene with Justin and make him desist from this proposal. Agapitus went to the East but obtained nothing. His attention was taken with problems of quite another kind. Once in the East he excommunicated the Patriarch Anthimus, the protege of Theodora, and forced him to resign. Menna, a Catholic, was consecrated in his place with the approval of Justin himself. But Agapito died suddenly just as he was about to return to Rome where his remains were transported and buried.

58. SILVERIUS, ST. (536-537)

A native of Campania, he was elected in great haste having been imposed by Theodahad who was in Rome awaiting the return of Agapito. Events precipitated. Theodahad was assassinated and the new king Vitige withdrew to organize for battle with Belisarius who had entered Italy and was marching on Rome. He entered the city shortly thereafter, invited by Pope Silverius. Despite his collaboration, Silverius had great trouble with the Empress Theodora who wanted to get even with Rome for the humiliation suffered at the hands of Pope Agapitus with regard to the archbishop of Constantinople. She knew that Silverius's ideas were the same as his predecessor's. Thus she set the Roman deacon Vigilius against him who aspired to the papacy and by ignoble subterfuges and false accusations induced Belisarius to depose and send him into exile. Silverius was sent to Lycia. Justin recognized his innocence and had him sent back to Rome, but he never got there. On new pretexts he was arrested and sent to the island of Ponza (Palmaria) where he died, possibly assassinated, and is buried. It appears that he renounced the papacy before his death.

59. VIGILIUS (537-555)

He was born in Rome of noble blood. His ascent to the papal throne was accomplished through simony and calumny as a result of the plot made against Silverius with the complicity of the Empress Theodora. Belisarius, instigated by his wife Antonia, had his election ratified. Vigilius had been made to promise Theodora that once he was pope he would restore the Eutychian Anthimus to the bishopric of Constantinople and revoke the condemnation of the monophysite theory pronounced by the council of Chalcedon. Asked to keep his promises, Vigilius first consented and revoked the condemnation. But when this provoked the ire of all the Western and African bishops, Vigilius retracted much to the annoyance of the Byzantine imperial court. Justin had him dragged by force to Constantinople where he was welcomed with great honors but was, in effect, a prisoner. The emperor demanded that the pope revoke the condemnation of the Eutychian doctrine. Then, even more than on other occasions, Vigilius showed the extent of his weakness by passing from one position to its exact opposite, thus antagonizing first one side, then the next. Vigilius's final decision was in favor of the Emperor Justin. To reward him for having finally done his will, Justin emanated the so-called <<Pragmatic Sanction>> with which the pope became associated with the Byzantine government in Italy and the bishops were given judicial powers as well as religious and civil ones. This doubtlessly strengthened the position of the Church with regard to the State. On the other hand, the emperor reserved the right to ratify the election of the Roman pope. Vigilius died at Syracuse on the return trip to Rome.

60. PELAGIUS I (556-561)

He was born in Rome. While Vigilius was away in the East, he remained in Rome and substituted for him with good results. He was elected a year after the latter's death. At first he was liked because of taking a more detached, consistent and firmer line towards Constantinople. But once elected pope, possibly to show thanks for the emperor's benevolence, he revoked the condemnation of Eutyche and accepted the decision of the council of Constantinople favoring the heresy. This about-face was a burden to him for the rest of his life and was never forgotten despite the fact that he later repeatedly disowned this momentary lapse and solemnly swore his total adhesion to the orthodox faith of the four ecumenical councils, especially the one of Chalcedon.
He made great efforts on behalf of the Roman populace and its indigent condition, making use of the prerogatives bestowed by Justin's <<Pragmatic Sanction>>.

61. JOHN III (561-574)

He was born in Rome of noble blood. During his pontificate the Longobards invaded Italy spreading death and terror: "...men fell as if mowed down by an unsheathed sword". The words come from Gregory the Great. Narses, who had replaced Belisarius, was called back to Constantinople by Justin II and Longinus sent in his place. Despite the emperor's good intentions, Italy remained badly defended against any foreign invader and without a valid regular army. The pope was impotent. John died just as the situation became dramatically desperate.

62. BENEDICT I (575-579)

A Roman, his brief pontificate was marked by the Longobard's siege of the city and the great famine undergone by the population within the walls. Links and communications with Constantinople were consequently cut and Rome was abandoned to itself.

63. PELAGIUS II (579-590)

Born in Rome, he may have been of Gothic extraction. His election did not receive the emperor's approvation simply because it was not reported. The Longobard's were still a great threat for Rome, even if the pressure and violence had attenuated thanks to the intervention of the Catholic Queen Theodolinda, wife of the new King Autaris. The Longobards, for the rest, were Arians. Pelagius, too, like his predecessor, had to face all the problems alone without the help of Constantinople. He tried appealing to the Franks, but in vain. Pelagius devoted himself to alleviating the discomfort and miseries of the poor and the old to whom he regularly gave shelter in his palace. He made dispositions for all priests to recite the Divine Office. He opposed and refused to recognize the title of "ecumenical" which the emperor had given to the archbishop of Constantinople. He died the victim of a terrible plague that arrived from Egypt and that decimated men and animals.

64. GREGORY I, ST. ("The Great") (590-604)

He was born in Rome to the noble Anicia family. He was prefect of Rome when, leaving a brilliant political career, he joined the Benedictine order whose rule he faithfully followed. He lived in privation and poverty, using his family's wealth to build monasteries. Pope Pelagius wanted him with himself, ordained him a deacon and sent him to Constantinople where he performed precious services for the Church. It was during those years that he became convinced that Rome was no longer interesting to Constantinople either for religious or political reasons. The seat of the papacy was abandoned to itself. On the death of Pelagius he was immediately elected pope. Thus Gregory did nothing but make note of Constaninople's lack of interest in Rome and Italy and he detached himself while reacquiring his autonomy as well as a clear and precise political and social connotation. In the absence of any political power, the Church remained the only point of reference for the Italian peoples and by a natural process it took on the role of guide and judge in both the temporal and religious spheres. Gregory used this new role - he was called "God's consul" - exclusively in the service of the Church and the people. He used the treasuries of the Church and the wealth of his own family to feed the people. He paid tribute to the Longobard King Agiluf, to call off the siege that for years had strangled the life of the city rendering it bitter and impossible. This initiative provoked criticism from the Emperor Maurice, who called him "a very poor diplomat". But Constantinople was only good at criticizing. He cleansed the papal court of all the laity and deacons who had been infesting it with the practice of simony, and in their place he put trusted and upright Benedictine monks. With the collaboration of Theodolinda he started a vast operation for the conversion of the Longobards to Catholicism. On that occasion he made her a gift of the Sacred Iron Crown that had been Constantine's and which today is conserved in the Monza Cathedral. He lavished the same fervor and work on the reorganizing of the liturgical life of the Church by reforming the Missal and reinforcing divine worship with the embellishment of the chants bearing his name and which still today are the basis of the solemn liturgical functions. He took continuous good care of the poor with whom he was in the habit of taking his meals. Many legends grew up around his figure. In some of them, besides himself, the angels appear as protagonists. For the sake of humility he liked to call himself "the servant of the servants of God" and from that moment on this description became a favorite attribute of the Roman pontiffs. His remains are conserved in the Cappella Clementina of St. Peter's Basilica.

65. SABINIAN (604-606)

Born in Tuscany, Gregory the Great sent him to Constantinople as papal nuncio. He did not follow his instructions so that the pope reprimanded and recalled him. This offended him greatly. Once he ascended the papal throne, he did everything to try discrediting Gregory, accusing him of doing good works just to attract attention and of having squandered the treasury of St. Peter even if with good intentions. Such loathing was also nourished by his jealousy in seeing how much the people loved and admired Gregory. The people noticed it and reproved him for it, but he persisted in this openly hostile attitude to his predecessor who was considered to be a saint and he ended by provoking the aversion and hatred of the people for himself. His death may have been a violent one.

66. BONIFACE III (607-607)

He was born in Rome but of Greek origin. He had been a friend of Gregory the Great who sent him as nuncio to Constantinople where he also enjoyed the esteem of the Emperor Phocas. When he became pope he obtained a declaration from the latter that only the bishop of Rome could call himself "ecumenical", which meant "universal". That is as much as is known of him.

67. BONIFACE IV (608-615)

Born in the region of Marsi (Latium), he was a Benedictine monk. He established the All Saints' Day holiday and concerned himself with the tenor of life and the education of the lower clergy. But the most significant event of his pontificate was the turning of the Pantheon from a pagan temple dedicated to all the gods into a Christian church dedicated to the Blessed Virgin and the Christian martyrs. For the occasion, Boniface filled the crypt under the altar with a large quantity of martyrs' bones taken from the catacombs. All this was possible thanks to the munificence of the Emperor Phocas who was anxious to ingratiate himself with the Roman populace and so granted Boniface's wish. History must thus thank Boniface with having saved one of the most beautiful and ingenious monuments of ancient Rome from certain destruction. The Romans returned the favor by erecting a memorial column to the emperor at the center of the Forum, a melancholy reminder of old splendors in a city which was now only a shadow of what it had been.

68. ADEODATUS I, ST. (615-618)

Born in Rome, he was the pontiff at a time when the desire was growing for independence from the Byzantine power which began to be felt more clearly and strongly as insufferable. At Ravenna, Naples and even in Rome there were rebellious movements while the territories governed by the Longobards were, by contrast, serene. Adeodatus or Deusdedit (as he had first been called) had the reputation of a healer who could cure the worst forms of plague merely by placing his lips on the suppurating sores of the stricken. His seal for official documents is known: it showed the Good Shepherd among the sheep and the bore the Christological symbols of alpha and omega. He was the first to use it. It is round, the size of a coin and in Latin is called *bulla*. He left a gift in silver for each cleric present at his burial.

69. BONIFACE V (619-625)

He was born in Naples. After his election he had to wait more than a year for imperial confirmation. There is not much known about him. The <<Liber pontificalis>> and his tombstone describe him as "very meek, benign, humble, tender and merciful" as well as "munificent, learned, chaste, sincere and just". He gave particular attention to the Anglo-Saxon Church as several of his writings attest, among which is a letter to the bishop Justus of Rochester and Canterbury and another to Ethelburga, queen of Kent. He established the right of asylum for anyone taking refuge in a church. During his pontificate, in 622, an extremely important event took place, the Hegira or the flight of Mohammed from Mecca and the beginning of his preaching. It is the first appearance of a great religion, Islam, with which the whole world would have to come to terms from this moment on.

70. HONORIUS I (625-638)

Born to a noble family in Campania, he succeeded in getting the clerics of the Church of Aquileia to rejoin the Church of Rome. Along with the Milan Church they had detached themselves because dissenting from Rome on the famous question of the Three Chapters of the council of Chalcedon which condemned the heresy of Eutiche. Honorius himself was accused of heresy for having written two letters to the Patriarch Sergius of Constantinople in which he approved the thesis of monoenergism (a single energy in Christ) thus moving close to monothelitism (a single will) which theory was wide spread in the Church, particularly in the East. The accusation and anathema were pronounced against him even by a council, the third one of Constantinople, after his death in (680). In his defense one may say that the letters cannot be considered dogmatic in character. Furthermore Honorius, in writing them, had only one goal in mind, that of resolving a practical question: an argument between Sergius and the monk Sophronius. In effect, the pope did not bother to go deeply into the matters he discussed, but only mentioned them in a cursory manner. To his credit, on the other hand, one must allow a noteworthy ability as an administrator of the treasury of the Holy See despite the large amounts spent on public works. It is enough to recall the reconstruction of the aqueduct of Trajan which brought water from Lake Bracciano to the Janiculum Hill, the restoration of the roof of St. Peter's Basilica and the transformation of many pagan buildings into Christian churches. He was much concerned with ecclesiastical discipline. In 638 Jerusalem fell under the domination of Islam.

71. SEVERINUS (640)

He was a Roman priest. His election was immediate but he could not be consecrated because the Emperor Heraclius would not approve him unless he ratified one of his edicts, the so-called *Echtesis* (profession of faith) which made monothelitism into an orthodox doctrine. Severino's messengers, sent to Constantinople to negotiate the matter, promised that the edict would be approved as soon as imperial recognition of the pope had been given. Not only did Severinus not approve the doctrine, but he had it condemned by a council. For revenge the emperor had the pontifical treasury plundered on false pretenses and accusations. Severinus died after a very short pontificate, possibly from vexation.

72. JOHN IV (640-642)

Except that he was born in Dalmatia, very little is known about him. He followed in the footsteps of his predecessors condemning the monothelitism and monoenergism of the Patriarch Sergius and defending the works and the memory of Pope Honorius. He probably gave money to his countrymen to help them rise from the oppressive conditions imposed on them by the Slavs. He had the bodies of three martyrs - Venantius, Anastasius and Maurus - brought to Rome and dedicated a chapel in the Lateran dedicated to them.

73. THEODORE I (642-649)

He was born in Jerusalem, but of Greek parents. He enjoyed the support of the Exarch Isaac of Ravenna who thought he had in him an ally in favor of monothelitism. But Theodore was opposed to it and condemned him. For the same error he condemned the Patriarch Peter of Constantinople and Pyrrhus who had been patriarch until deposed by Heraclius. Pyrrhus came to Rome to seek the support of the pope, declaring that he was orthodox and disowning his monothelite beliefs. Then, when he saw that Theodore could not help him, he retracted everything and returned to monothelitism and to Constantinople. The new Emperor Constans II, tired of all this, abolished the *Echtesis*, which was the document that triggered so many disputes, and issued a new edict, the *Typos*, by which he prohibited everyone, including the pope, to deal in theological matters, and in particular those regarding the double or single will of the two natures of Christ. In substance, everyone was allowed to believe what he liked, but discussion was not allowed. This edict, rather than quieting things down, only fired up the conflicts, aggravating them and resolving nothing. Theodore died before ever having set eyes on the *Typos*.

74. MARTIN I, ST. (649-655)

He was born at Todi in Umbria. He was consecrated without waiting for the emperor's recognition. He immediately concerned himself with the serious problem of the monothelite heresy that was dividing the Church. He called a council in the Lateran at which about one hundred bishops were present and which condemned Sergius, Peter and Pyrrhus, patriarchs of Constantinople, and the *Echtesis* of Heraclius and the *Typos* of Constans.

That is when Martin's troubles began. The Emperor Constans took it personally and sent the Exarch Olympius to Rome to take Martin prisoner and bring him to Constantinople. There Martin was subjected to an infamous and humiliating trial, but he did not give in. He continued to defend the orthodox creed despite humiliations, suffering and a death sentence. He was pardoned and exiled to Chersonesus in the Crimea after being deposed. He died in exile, abandoned by all, even the Roman clergy which did not oppose this outrageous abuse. Martin was rightly considered a martyr of both the Eastern and Western Churches. He was first buried in Constantinople and then removed to the Church of San Martino ai Monti in Rome.

75. EUGENE I, St. (654-657)

Born in Rome, he was elected on the express wish of Emperor Constans one year before the death of Martin as the latter was being led in chains to Constantinople. Neither Eugene nor the rest of the Roman clergy opposed the will of Constans, probably not because of fear or submission, but from opportunism. Perhaps no one wanted to irritate the emperor who could have had, for example, a Monothelite pope elected; or perhaps by showing themselves to be accomodating, they hoped to keep from worsening the already precarious position of Pope Martin. There is no doubt that the Eugene's behavior was too weak and accomodating, to the point where the *Liber pontificalis* called it too "benevolent, soft and tame". He rehabilitated himself towards the end by rejecting a synodical letter sent to him by the Patriarch Peter which contained serious doctrinal ambiguities of a monothelite nature and refusing to sign a profession of faith dictated by the emperor himself. On the contrary, he reacted to the provocation by denouncing the abuses and persecutions that Pope Martin had been subjected to by the imperial court, thus making them public. He would most certainly have received the same treatment as his predecessor if he had not died first. He prescribed perpetual chastity for priests.

76. VITALIAN, ST. (657-672)

Born at Segni in Latium, his pontificate coincided with the apex of the monothelite heresy's expansion when Emperor Constans II came to Rome. The pope received him with great honors and he visited the basilicas with an air of touching and edifying devoutness, but it was all just for show. On leaving Rome he authorized it to be infamously sacked and took an enormous load of booty away with him. Immediately afterwards he agreed to the request of Maurus, the bishop of Ravenna, for independence from Rome and established the regulation that from then on the bishop should receive the pallium from Constantinople and not from Rome as was already the case for the Eastern patriarch. His intention was evident to detach Ravenna from Rome in order to limit the papal power in Italy. Vitalian excommunicated Maurus, but the latter remained firm in his intention and for about ten years the Ravenna Church remained separated from Rome. When Constans died at Syracuse, Vitaliano gave support to his son Constans, defending him against the pretender Mezezius who was backed by the army. When Constans became Constantine IV the new emperor showed unconditional gratitude to Vitalian and adopted a more prudent religious policy and greater respect for the Roman papacy. So there was peace between Rome and Constantinople. Vitalian wrote several letters to the English King Oswin and sent papal nunzios to all parts of Europe.

77. ADEODATUS II (672-676)

Born in Rome, he was a monk in the monastery of San Erasmo al Celio. Very little is known about him. He too had supported the Emperor Constantine IV against the pretender Mezezius thus winning the emperor's esteem. The epistolary formula *salutem et apostolicam benedictionem* goes back to him. On the whole his pontificate enjoyed relative tranquillity. That was the time when the conversion of the Moronites began whereas a new danger was threatening Christianity: the Saracens. Having been repelled at the siege of Constantinople (673), the Saracens landed in Sicily and occupied Syracuse. Adeodatus granted the Venetians the right to elect their own doge.

78. DONUS (676-678)

Born in Rome he had a quiet papacy protected by the friendship and collaboration of the Emperor Constantine IV who in a letter called him "ecumenical pope". During his papacy the schism with Ravenna was overcome. The new Archbishop Theodore deferred to the pope, renouncing all claims of independence, thanks in part to the intervention of the emperor who actually proposed to the pope a theological conference among Eastern and Western bishops to resolve the divergences that still divided the Churches. Donus supported the establishment of two schools that in the future were to become famous cultural centers: Cambridge and Triers.

79. AGATHO, ST. (678-681)

Possibly born at Palermo or, according to some, at Reggio Calabria, he was famous as a healer and it seems was almost one hundred years old at the time of his election. He granted the request that Emperor Constantine IV had made to Donus to convene a theological conference sent a delegation to Constantinople bearing a "profession of faith" that Constantine submitted to a council of 170 bishops. The council, with the emperor presiding, condemned monothelitism and monoenergism at the same time as it reaffirmed the doctrine that in Christ there are two natures and two corresponding wills, one divine and one human. This council is known as the Trullan Council, the name taken from the shape of the cupola surmounting the hall where it was held. Agatho managed to get exemption from the tax of three thousand scudi imposed by Justinian as payment for imperial recognition every time a pope was elected. He sent singing teachers to England to teach the new Gregorian chants. He probably lived to be 107 years old.

80. LEO II, ST. (682-683)

Born in Catania, he confirmed the decisions of the Council of Constantinople and had them translated into Greek from Latin, and not omitting to note the error of Pope Honorius who neglected to take an immediate position against the monothelite heresy "as a pope should have done". For this Honorius was condemned and excommunicated "post mortem" during the course of the same council. Leo, even while recognizing the justice of the council's document, still defended Pope

Honorius's actions, justifying them by tracing them back to the particular situation which caused them. He asked Emperor Constantine IV to issue a decree establishing the norms for the consecration of the bishop of Ravenna. It was in any case to take place in Rome and only after an act of submission to the pope. He introduced holy water into Christian rites and ordered them to be celebrated with great splendor. He also introduced "the kiss of peace" into the mass.

81. BENEDICT II, ST. (684-685)

He was born in Rome to the powerful Savelli family and was so esteemed by Emperor Constantine IV that the latter had him adopt his two sons Justinian and Heraclius. The same emperor granted the Roman Church and people greater autonomy, giving them the right to elect the pope without having to have the emperor's approval as Justinian had established. The exarch of Ravenna was given this task. Very probably it was Benedict who convinced the emperor to make this modification.

82. JOHN V (685-686)

He was born at Antioch in Syria. He may have been elected on the suggestion of the Emperor Constantine IV Pogonatus. However, very little is known about him. He was a cardinal deacon and a representative of Pope Agatho to the Trullan Council in Constantinople where monothelitism and monoenergism were condemned. He may have been the one to deprive the archbishop of Cagliari of the right to consecrate bishops and transfer it to Rome.

83. CONON (686-687)

It is not known where he came from, but before coming to Rome he had been educated in Sicily. There he was ordained both as priest and bishop. His election was a surprise and an expediency to overcome the contention of two other more prominent candidates. Endowed with great goodness and charity, he helped the monasteries and the clergy in general. The exarch of Ravenna renewed the usage of imperial approval for newly elected popes as Emperor Constantine IV had disposed and he could not oppose the decision. He may have died by poisoning.

84. SERGIUS I, ST. (687-701)

Of Syrian origin, he may have been born in Sicily. Two others were elected together with him, but the disagreement was short lived and he was able to govern in peace with the approval of the Exarch John Platyn of Ravenna. He managed to resolve a rift between Rome and the Armenian Church. But he had an intense conflict with the new Emperor Justinian II. The emperor had a council convened in his palace without the pope's consent which is known as the Quinisext Council. Pope Sergius had not even been invited. But the 102 propositions were submitted to him for his approval and signature. The pope, of course, refused to sign, so Justinian ordered his arrest. The imperial edict was universally held to be sacrilege for the first time and so aroused a general rebellion. Even Ravenna, the Pentapolis and the bordering provinces, indignant, sent their armies to defend the pope along with the Roman people. For Justinian this affair ended his power and his physical integrity. He was dethroned, mutilated and sent into exile. Contrarily, it was a factor that began a great consolidation of the pope's power. It became ever more evident that he was the prime master of Italy. Under his pontificate there was a definitive resolution of the problem of the Three Chapters of the council of Chalcedon regarding the Eutichian heresy. He baptized the Saxon King Caedwalla in St. Peter's on Easter Saturday 689. He introduced the triple chanting of Agnus Dei during the mass. He gave support to Venice as part of his effort to become independent of Constantinople.

85. JOHN VI (701-705)

He may have been born at Ephesus and he too had to fight against the Eastern emperor who on various pretexts tried to interfere in religious matters with the exarch of Ravenna as his tool. John always offered energetic opposition even on an occasion when the exarch came to Rome with hostile intentions. The new emperor was repeating the same error that Justinian II made with regard to Pope Sergius: that is to say, he wanted to take John prisoner. And as on that previous occasion there was a general rebellion in defence of the pope so that the exarch's attempt failed completely. The Italic peoples behaved less and less like subjects of the Eastern empire, feeling themselves more bound to the pope who was seen as the new natural depository of power.

86. JOHN VII (705-707)

He was of Greek origin. Justinian II had returned to power in Constantinople and did everything to regain control of Italy too. But his project was destined to fail both because of the resistance of John and the hostility to Byzantium of the Italic peoples who were experiencing "nationalistic" feelings. And this feeling was taking conscious form along with the idea of the papacy as the institution with which to oppose Constantinople.

87. SISSINIUS (708-708)

Of Syrian origin, he lasted only twenty days. He was very ill and suffered from gout. He had enough time to begin collecting funds for the restoration of the city walls against a possible invasion of the Longobards who were a constant threat to Rome. His only documented official act was the ordaining of a bishop for Corsica.

88. CONSTANTINE (708-715)

Born in Syria, unlike his predecessors, he had good relations with the Emperor Justinian II. He went to Constantinople to iron out several questions pertaining to the last council held there, the Trullan Council. The emperor received him with great honors confirming the privileges of the Church and the obligation of the bishop of Ravenna to make submission to the pope. But his aim was to obtain from the pope some concessions of doctrine regarding monothelitism. He did not succeed. Not much time passed and Justinian was killed by Philippicus Bardanes who proclaimed himself emperor. He tried to get the approval of the pope for this act, but Constantine, considering him a monothelite heretic, refused to recognize him. The parts had become inverted: now it was the emperor who asked for recognition from the Roman pontiff. And this was a fact of extreme importance, as was Constantine's refusal for the events it provoked: there was an almost immediate rebellion against Philippicus who was deposed by Anastasius II, one of his ministers. Anastasius proclaimed himself emperor, saying that he was orthodox, respectful of the pope and of the decisions of the Sixth or Trullan Council. Constantine could not enjoy the fruits of this capitulation because he died too soon. But he strengthened the position of the Church for the benefit of his successors.

89. GREGORY II, ST. (715-731)

He was born in Rome to the Savelli family. The true temporal power of the papacy begins with him inasmuch as a territorial nucleus was formed which will develop into the Papal State. The new Emperor of the East, Leo III the Isaurian, made a decree prohibiting sacred images and ordering that they be destroyed by fire (iconoclasm). Gregory immediately opposed this with the support of the clergy and all Christian peoples not subject to the Greeks. He convened a council which condemned iconoclasm and issued a bull prohibiting the emperor to legislate in matters of faith. Leo responded by way of the exarch of Ravenna who sent an army against Rome, threatening to take the pope prisoner. Rebellions arose everywhere against Ravenna's troops. At this point another figure intervened: Liutprand, king of the Longobards, who supported the rebellions hoping to win an advantage from them against both Rome and Ravenna. His intention was, in fact, to make himself master of Italy. He conquered Ravenna and made straight for Rome. Venice and the duchies of Spoleto and Benevento, ready for battle, came to the aid of the pope menaced on two fronts. Liutprand stopped at the gates of Rome. But it was not so much the armies of the pope's allies to make him give up his intent. Rather it was Gregory himself, strong in his spiritual authority, who convinced him and forced Liutprand to prostrate himself at his feet and render him obeisance. At this point the Lombard king tried everything to ingratiate himself with the pope and take the place of the Eastern emperor. He dedicated the town of Sutri to "Saints Peter and Paul" and other territories that he had won from the Greeks. This first nucleus was called the *Ducato romano* (Roman Duchy). Aside from politics, in which he was brilliant, Gregory must be remembered for his pastoral work: he gave a strong impulse to monachism which had slowed down. He began with the reconstruction of the Abbey of Montecassino. He also undertook the intensive evangelization of the Germanic peoples.

90. GREGORY III, ST. (731-741)

Born in Syria, it is said that he was acclaimed pope while the funeral of Gregory II was still under way. He was one of the popes beloved by the Roman people. With regard to Constantinople he followed in the footsteps of his predecessors. He convened a council at St. Peter's in which iconoclasm was condemned. He also wrote severe epistles to Emperor Leo III the Isaurian notifying him of the condemnation and illustrating his thoughts on the relations between Church and Empire which had to be marked by reciprocal independence as had been formulated by Pope Gregory II. More so, the pope enjoyed supremacy in relation to the emperor. He had to fight against the Longobards over territorial questions. Liutprand felt defrauded by Gregory's expansionistic policy, for which reason, forgetting his earlier act of submission and his promises, he began repeatedly invading and raiding the territories of the *Ducato*. Thus the pope had recourse to Charles Martell, king of the Franks. The latter, being related to the Longobards and for other political reasons, did not accept the pope's request to fight against them. But he offered other kinds of support, primarily in religious matters. In fact, he furnished the monk Boniface with a safe-conduct pass and various aid in his attempt to evangelize the Germans. Nevertheless to Gregory must go the credit for having intuited and earmarked a people, the Franks, who not much later would bind their fortunes and their history with that of the Church. He was responsible too for establishing a kind of charity fund, requesting the Christians of almost all of Europe to send offerings to Rome for charitable works. It was a kind of taxation, certainly not imposed with force, but morally obligatory.

91. ZACHARIAS, ST. (741-752)

Either from Greece or from Magna Grecia, he was a Benedictine monk. The Church territories were constantly being disturbed and raided by the Longobard troops. Zacharias could expect no help either from the Emperor Artabardus, who cared nothing about Italy, nor from the Franks who were occupied with problems pertaining to the succession after the death of Charles Martell. So there was nothing left for him to do but confront Liutprand. He managed a reconciliation with him and, during a memorable banquet, stipulated a 20-year peace pact with him. This pact was a true masterpiece. Liutprand gave Zacharias new territories other than those previously ceded. But Pope Zacharias's political skill went beyond this first success. He accomplished a second masterpiece. Liutprand himself and his successor Aistulf gave him the opportunity by not keeping to the pact and once more invading the Pentapolis and Ravenna. Thus the Longobards were not to be trusted. Zacharias, looking for a reliable ally to defend the territories of the Church, thought of the Franks and Pepin III who was the de facto administrator of the Frankish state even if he had not yet been consecrated as king. The legitimate king was Childeric III to whom Pepin had sworn fidelity. Pepin would have liked to supplant Childeric, but he was torn by doubts. He turned to the pope asking him if it were just to undermine one's king and put oneself in his place, beginning a new dynasty. Zacharias resolved his perplexities by replying that it were better if the title of king pertained to the one who effectively held power and not to him who had lost it. In thus saying, he consented to Pepin's coronation. Zacharias obtained a double advantage: he immediately found a good and reliable ally, and he established a tradition that would go on for centuries. From that moment on the pope became the almost unopposed arbiter of European politics. Zacharias died shortly thereafter and was buried in the Vatican grottoes.

92. STEPHEN II (III) (752-757)

Born in Rome, he continued the policy of rapprochement with the Franks that had been started by Gregory III and Zacharias. The occasion was presented to him by the new king of the Longobards, Aistulf, who had invaded Ravenna and other papal territories without keeping faith with the pact Liutprand had stipulated with Pope Zacharias. Thus Stephen travelled to France to ask for the intervention of Pepin III. He crowned him as sovereign and named him "Roman patrician" as thanks for his donations and aid to the Church. This was tantamount to a solemn pledge and promise from Pepin to come to the defence of the Church and of Rome against the Longobards. But Pope Stephen's real aim was something else: to exploit Pepin's friendship and the military power of the Franks to create an extended Papal State with precise and well protected borders. For the pope this was an inalienable right sanctioned even by a document in the possession of the Church, the famous *Constitutum Costantini* or the Donation of Constantine. The document spoke of a gift by the Emperor Constantine to Pope Silvester and the Roman Church of a well-defined territory and, above all, of dominion over Italy and all the West. The document had been definitely shown to be false, but Pepin thought it was genuine and he solemnly committed himself to it. Furthermore the commitment was addressed to St. Peter himself and not only to the pope. Pepin travelled to Italy twice. On both occasions he defeated Aistulf and restored the occupied territories to the pope. On the second occasion he also consigned to Stephen the Exarchate of Ravenna. The papal territories were increasing. Stephen was carried in triumph by the Romans to the Lateran. That was when the usage of the gestatorial chair started. Stephen was a determined, cunning and clever pope. What he could not get by persuasion he got by threats. Still famous is his invitation to Pepin to return to Rome a second time on pain of excommunication and hell fire. He died at the height of his powers.

93. PAUL, ST. (757-767)

Born in Rome, he was the brother of Stephen II and was elected during his brother's last days of life. As soon as elected, he took care to inform Pepin of the fact as had once been done with the emperor of the East. Paul still had need of Pepin because Desiderius, the successor of Aistulf, had not yet given back the papal territories that had been taken. The situation remained suspended for another while. Paul tried to take up contact with the Greek Church once more, making a show of friendship and willingness. For his part, Emperor Constantine V ignored the pope and tried to make a pact directly with Pepin, proposing, among other things, that he receive and spread in the West the decisions of a council held in Constantinople that condemned the veneration of holy images. Pepin did not consider the proposal for a moment. On the contrary, he showed absolute fidelity to the pope by calling a council to expressly approve such veneration. The emperor in reality was trying to create a division between the pope and the king of the Franks to prepare the way for reconquering the Italian territories which had once belonged to Constantinople. The question of Desiderius was somehow resolved with the reciprocal restitution of territories and cities.

94. STEPHEN III (IV) (768-772)

Born at Syracuse in Sicily, two other popes had been designated before him. The first, Philipp, withdrew of his own volition one day after his nomination. The second, Constantine, was a layman imposed by force of arms and who, following riots, would end in prison and be killed. The papacy had begun to be considered a temporal power to all effects which made many mouths water, including those of laymen. To overcome the obstacle of being ordained in the clergy, the aspiring layman need only have a conniving bishop at his disposition or one who could be convinced by force at the right moment. To put a stop to this perilous tendency, a council was held in the Lateran where, with several French bishops present, it was established that no layman could be elected pope if he had not first been a cardinal. It was in the course of this council that Constantine was put on trial, condemned, ill-treated and thrashed before being sentenced to death. In politics Stephen was utterly ambiguous now seeking rapprochement with the Franks and now with the Longobards. In the end he bound himself more and more tightly to the Franks. He urgently advised their King Pepin not to give his two sons in marriage to the two daughters of Desiderius. This advice was not heeded, but he turned out to be a good prophet.

95. HADRIAN I (772-795)

Born in Rome to the noble Colonna family. During his pontificate the star of Charlemagne rose and shone. The two sons of Pepin III, Charles and Carloman, had married the daughters of Desiderius, Irmengard and Gerberga. When Carloman died, his widow Gerberga was deposed while Charles repudiated Irmengard. This gave Desiderius a reason to invade the Pentapolis and part of the Exarchate of Ravenna on the excuse that the pope had not defended Gerberga's rights nor adequately opposed the repudiation of Irmengard. Hadrian then summoned Charles to Italy who came at once and defeated Desiderius various times finally taking Desiderius and his family prisoner. This put an end to the Longobard domination of Italy. As a result Charles was given the title Charlemagne (Charles the Great), was received in Rome with great honors and named a "Roman patrician". Thus putting the "patrminoy of St. Peter" under his protection which he extended by adding more territories to it. Charles entrusted the governing of Italy to his son Pepin who was crowned by the pope and had his capital at Pavia. Hadrian governed the Church for a long time, 23 years, and did much to its benefit. He had numerous diplomatic successes: apart from his solidarity with Charlemagne, he had excellent relations with the Byzantine Empress Irene who helped renew the veneration of sacred images. But his main merits were the intensive building activity and what today would be called an agrarian reform and policy which increased the work, wealth and well being of the citizens. In fact, he promoted the revival of land cultivation around Rome, which had been abandoned under the Longobards, and had the produce brought to the Lateran where it was distributed to the poor. He reconstructed and put back into service many of the old imperial aqueducts. He had the city walls reinforced which had been partially destroyed by the Longobards. He began a grandiose restoration of the Roman churches that changed the look of the city so much that some have spoken of "Hadrian's Rome". It is to him that one owes the construction of the Santo Spirito Hospital which still functions today. So vast a program, territorial defence, the poor to be fed, called for such large financial resources that Hadrian was always on the look out for funds. That may be the reason he was accused of being too attached to money. Another accusation made aganst him was that of nepotism. Why?

96. LEO III, ST. (795-816)

Born in Rome, his election was opposed by two relatives of Hadrian who were also aiming at the pontificate. They went so far as to take him prisoner, but the populace freed him. Not feeling safe, however, he went to France where he asked for and was granted Charlemagne's help. He then returned to Rome where he was received in triumph and restored to the papal throne. It was the year 800. On Christmas Eve of that year a memorable historical event took place which would have great effect on political and social life: in St. Peter's Basilica, Pope Leo crowned Charlemagne as emperor with the famous dedication: "Long life and victory to the most pious and august Charles, crowned by God, great and peaceful emperor". Thus the Holy Roman Empire was born, the continuation of the Western Roman Empire with its seat at Aix-la-Chapelle. The emperor became the protector and guarantor of the safety and interests of the pope and the Church, reserving for himself the approval of the election of the pope. For his part, the pope granted France the title of "first-born daughter of the Church". This same action marked the deep and definitive break with Constantinople which felt authorized, both Church and empire, to attack Rome on the level of politics and doctrine. Constantinople had, in fact, been excluded from Western politics. The Roman Church had made a choice: to promote the birth of the new European empire and to opt for its own security, but making an enemy of the East. Europe had a new administrative structure: counties and regions were created governed and controlled by *missi dominici* which were directly answerable to the emperor. In general these were bishops. Charlemagne made many donations to the clergy and established schools in the monasteries. He founded the famous Palatine School, the first nucleus of the University of Paris. Leo died two years after the emperor and was buried in St. Peter's Basilica.

97. STEPHEN IV (V) (816-817)

Born in Rome of a noble family, he did not bother to notify Charlemagne's son, the new emperor, Louis the Pious, of his election immediately. But in compensation he went to Reims to crown the emperor and his consort Irmengard. In so doing he meant to emphasize that he was the spiritual leader while the emperor's job was political. Louis indicated his acceptance of pope's position and during the ceremony prostrated himself three times before him to show his spiritual submission. Furthermore, he confirmed all of the Church's previously held privileges and accorded it his protection. For his part, Stephen, conscious that social peace was necessary to govern well, tried to resolve the differences among the conflicting parities in Rome by granting, for example, pardon to those who had opposed the election of Leo III and restoring them to their offices. He never got to see the fruits of this pacification since he died very soon.

98. PASCHAL I, ST. (817-824)

He was born in Rome of the Massimo family. The good relations between the Church and the Franks continued and grew stronger. Louis the Pious gave the pope Corsica and Sardinia. The pope in return crowned Louis' son Lothair king of Italy and recognizing his authority over the Romans as equal to what had been that of the Byzantine emperors in the past. Paschal excommunicated the Eastern Emperor Leo V who had once more begun iconoclastic persecutions and at the same time he gave donations in support of those Christians who were subjects of Islam. He was a devout and fervent venerator of the martyrs. He had their relics dug up in great quantities and conserved in many churches. In particular, he uncovered the remains of St. Cecilia in the Catacombs of San Callisto and had them moved to the church dedicated to her. He had been considered a saint before his election and continued to be venerated as such after his death.

99. EUGENE II (824-827)

Born in Rome, his nomination was greeted with riotous disorder. In particular, the priest Lyssinius opposed him and proposed himself. He sent messengers to Louis the Pious to inform him of his election. Hearing of the serious disorders, the emperor sent his son Lothair to Rome who did his best to placate and bring peace to the opposing factions. In agreement with Eugene he wrote a "Roman Constitution" which established some legal principles to be employed in resolving any controversies. This constitution provided for the relations between the papacy and the empire and between these and their subjects. The substance of it was that the two powers needed each other. But in this balance of power the papacy seems to have lost a few points and fell under the control of Aix-la-Chapelle as it had fallen under that of Constantinople before. Eugene formed a commission to keep check on the application of the laws. This group was the origin of the Roman curia. It was also concerned with the education of the people. Eugene died at a time when his relations with Louis were deteriorating.

100. VALENTINE (827-827)

He was born in Rome in the vicinity of Via Lata. All that is known of him is that he swore the oath that Lothair dictated to him and that he was much liked by the Romans as a good and virtuous man. His pontificate lasted about a month. He is buried in the Vatican Grottoes.

101. GREGORY IV (827-844)

Born in Rome of a noble family. He tried to refuse the election in view of the grave problems that existed: quarrels and hard battles at the imperial court and the Saracens who were the masters of the seas bringing terror and death. The controversies at the imperial court regarded the division of the empire. Gregory travelled to France in the attempt to resolve them. He did not succeed. A solution was found only after the death of Louis the Pious and that of the pope (844). A treaty was signed at Verdun which gave Italy to Lothair, France to Charles II and Gaul and Germany to Louis the German. The Saracen pirates were a menace to Italy and Rome. They landed ever more often at Ostia threatening Rome from close by. To defend the city Gregory built a fortress and a town on the sea which he called Gregoropolis. He definitively fixed November 1 as the date of All Saints Day.

102. SERGIUS II (844-847)

Born in Rome, his election was contested by the deacon John who was elected by his own followers but was immediately considered an anti-pope. The latter was so determined in his intent that he went as far as to attack Sergius in the Lateran Basilica. In his relations with the Carolingian empire, Sergius aimed at reinforcing the pope's autonomy even while being very careful not to cause fractures. He crowned Louis II king of Italy, the son of Lothair who had in the meantime become king of France. During his pontificate the Saracens landed at Ostia and made camp there. Then they continued on to Rome without meeting any resistance and sacked the basilicas of St. Peter and St. Paul (846). The fortified village built at Ostia by Gregory IV precisely against such an event had in the meantime been abandoned and so served no purpose whatever. Famine was added to the terror caused by the pirates. In these circumstances the shepherd soul of Sergius came to the fore and he dedicated himself completely to alleviating the sufferings of the people, thus redeeming a pontificate which some historians find burdened with quite a few dark sides. Sergius had the Holy Stairs set up near the Lateran which tradition says St. Helen had brought from Palestine.

103. LEO IV, ST. (847-855)

He was born in Rome even if a Longobard in origin. His name is connected with the construction of the so-called "Leonine city", a fortification that surrounded the Vatican hill and encompassed the basilica of St. Peter, the palaces and the settlement that had arisen around the Castel Sant'Angelo. This construction, which had been thought up by Pope Sergius and Lothair was urgently needed in defence against the raids of the Saracens which was a constant threat for Rome. To fight off the pirates a league had been formed by Amalfi, Gaeta and Naples to which Louis also adhered. The pope himself, supported by the nobles of Campania, took up arms and departed. The Saracens were defeated and Leo showed his gratitude by crowning Louis emperor. A miracle has been attributed to Pope Leo which took place during one of the Saracen's raids. A raging fire broke out and was destroying the village. The pope succeeded in extinguishing it by going to the window and displaying an icon of the Blessed Virgin Mary. This scene has been immortalized in one of Raphael's frescos in his Stanze and is entitled "Fire in the village". But Leo did not concern himself with Saracens and wars alone. He also had to do with schisms and errors of doctrine which he always energetically opposed. He was the first pope to indicate on his official documents the year of his papacy. He introduced the rite of sprinkling holy water on persons and objects to bless them and purify them.

104. BENEDICT III (855-858)

Born in Rome, his rival for the papacy was a certain Anastasius called "the librarian", a choleric and greedy man who took the papal throne by deceit and force but remained in office only a month. Benedict was a learned and generous pope who dedicated himself primarily to charitable work for the poor and the sick and to reawakening the moral sense that society had lost. He pardoned Anastasius, who had had him imprisoned, and even gave him a church. He is buried in the Vatican Grottoes. Between Leo IV and Benedict was inserted the famous "Pope Joan" of which the *Universal Chronicle of Metz* speaks. By now it is clear that this story and personage were invented from beginning to end.

Italy, France and Germany. The title of emperor was given to Guido, duke of Spoleto, who had helped the pope fight the Saracens. The pope retained the right to crown the emperor even if this was only a formality held in Rome. With the disappearance of central power, that of the small and large feudal lords grew. The influence and wealth of several bishops grew as well, to whom the feudal lords entrusted their territories, not being able to defend them against the attacks of the barbarians. Stephen was an intelligent man and fostered the arts and crafts. He abolished the practice of trial by fire because it tempted God.

111. FORMOSUS (891-896)

He was either from Rome or Ostia. His was a sad destiny: during his life he was persecuted and after his death put on trial and profaned. It will be remembered that he was deposed unjustly by John VIII from his bishop's seat at Porto and subsequently reinstated by John's successor Marinus. His election coincided with a turbulent period in which opposing factions fought ruthlessly. Immediately after his election he crowned Guido of Spoleto and his son Lambert. But they turned against him and Formosus saw himself obliged to seek help from Arnulf of Carinthia, who rushed to his defence. From gratitude, Formosus crowned him too. These inconsistencies, obviously induced by opportunism or fear, only increased disagreement and malcontent, thus focusing such hatred upon him that it provoked a horrible action of an unheard of kind and, most astonishingly of all, upon a corpse. After Formosus' death, the new Pope Stephen VI, a friend of the duke of Spoleto, unearthed his corpse, put it on trial, mutilated it, and had it thrown into the Tiber. Merciful hands salvaged it and buried it at St. Peter's.

112. BONIFACE VI (896-896)

He was born either in Rome or in Tuscany. The people elected him by acclamation having been nominated by the faction favoring the dukes of Spoleto. His was a very short pontificate - fifteen days - and a turbulent one. Those days saw the beginning of a sad period for the papacy in the clutches of the powerful Roman patrician families who, for various reasons, tried to influence the elections of the popes, and once getting them elected, to condition their actions.

113. STEPHEN VI (896-897)

Born in Rome, he was elected thanks to the influence of the duke of Spoleto. With his election the turbulence and disorders ceased, but certainly not because of any merits or moral qualities of his which, on the contrary, were entirely questionable. Rather it was because the Spoleto party had the city under control and had no rivals. The price the pope had to pay for such protection was very high: he was forced to convene a synod and hold a post-mortem trial of his predecessor Formosus, guilty of having sought the help of Arnulf of Carinthia to defend himself from the overbearing force of Guido of Spoleto. Stephen, as has been said, had the corpse of Formosus exhumed, and put on trial in a most ignominious, ignoble and barbarous way. The corpse was mutilated (the three fingers he had used for blessing were cut off) and his dismembered body thrown into the Tiber. His memory was condemned, all his acts declared null and void including the priests he had ordained. Some have called Stephen the worst pope in history up to that time. This and other actions earned him the hatred of the people. Instigated by the deposed priests, they took justice into their own hands. Stephen was arrested and strangled. But his remains were not profaned and he was buried in the Vatican Grottoes.

114. ROMANUS (897-897)

Born at Gallese in Latium, he had been a friend of Pope Formosus, for which reason he had his memory rehabilitated by annulling the decisions taken by the synod over which Stephen VI had presided. He confirmed the authority of the Church of Gerona over the islands of Mallorca and Minorca. His pontificate was most brief and little is known of him, not even of the way he died. Some have talked of poisoning, and some of his being obliged to end his days in a monastery after having been deposed.

115. THEODORE II (897-897)

He was a Roman or perhaps Greek. Twenty days was the length of his papacy. He had the time to call a synod to rehabilitate the memory of Pope Formosus and, consequently, all the acts of his pontificate. Then he concerned himself with giving a dignified burial the unhappy pope's remains which had meanwhile been fished out of the Tiber. In Theodore's case too, there is talk of poisoning.

116. JOHN IX (898-900)

He was from Tivoli. He confirmed the rehabilitation of Pope Formosus. At the same time he called a council which exiled and excommunicated all those cardinals who were accomplices of Stephen VI in the "synod of the corpse". Meanwhile he recalled and restored to their offices those bishops and priests who had been expelled simply because ordained by Formosus. During the same council, which was held at Ravenna with the participation of 74 bishops and the consent of the Roman people and patricians, it was decided that an imperial representative had to be present at papal elections to guarantee order and validity. Agreements were also made with Lambert of Spoleto, who was crowned emperor and king of Italy, to take on the task of protecting the Church and the pope so that the latter could perform his pontifical ministry. But Lambert died very soon and Italy fell back into anarchy. In that year of 898 North Italy was invaded by ferocious and bloody Hungarians, who plundered and devastated the land, abbeys and monasteries in particular.

117. BENEDICT IV (900-903)

A Roman of indubitable generosity and virtue, he was at the same time certainly not up to the immense task to which he had been called in a time of atrocious violence: the Hungarians in the North, the Saracens in the South, and Rome always more at the mercy of uncontrolled greed and rapacity on the part of the families and lords who alternated in power by means of constant coups that bloodied, robbed and humiliated the city. Benedict sought respite from all this by conferring the imperial crown on

124. STEPHEN VII (VIII) (928-931)

A Roman, he too was a creature of Marozia, but was a good and peaceful man. Several monasteries were in debt to him for the privileges he granted them. He was buried in the Vatican Grottoes. Apropos of the popes who were elected thanks to Marozia and her intrigues, one should note that they had two characteristics in common: they were generally men of a good and peaceful nature, which is to say they were weak and did not oppose her, nor did they last long. If nature did not collaborate in putting an end to their lives, she saw to it.

125. JOHN XI (931-935)

He was a Roman of the counts of Tuscolo family and the son of Marozia and Alberic I. It was his powerful mother who arranged for him to be elected. In the meantime she had gone on to her third marriage, this time with the Emperor Hugh of Provence. John was barely 25 and was unsuitable both by age and experience to face the intricate situation of that violent epoch as well as being too weak to deal with such greedy and unscrupulous personages. The situation became very heavy going for him and involved him emotionally as well in a total and fatal way. His brother, Alberic II, son of Marozia and Alberic I, tired of the vexations caused by Hugh of Provence, aroused the people against him and had him chased out of the city. He then had himself proclaimed prince and senator of Rome. For her part, Marozia was imprisoned. Then, profiting from the ineptitude of his brother John, he took away all his authority and had him imprisoned too. He governed the Church himself, barely leaving the pope with the religious questions. In such conditions, John devoted himself to monastic reform, thus supporting the work of St. Odo of Cluny and helping him to spread it. John was only thirty when he died and is buried in St. John Lateran.

126. LEO VII (936-939)

A Roman, he became pope probably due to the influence of Alberic II. He esteemed the Roman senator so that they came to an agreement: Alberic was to have civil power and the pope religious power. Leo had been a Benedictine monk and so his main interest was for reorganizing the monasteries in collaboration with St. Odo of Cluny, thus continuing the work of his predecessor. Among other things, he rebuilt the monastery of St. Paul's outside the walls. He made great efforts to bring clarity to religious issues by warning the bishops and the clergy of the dangers of witchcraft which was spreading widely. He solemnly excommunicated witches and sorcerers.

127. STEPHEN VIII (IX) (939-942)

Born in Rome, or according to others in Germany, he was elected pope after the death of Leo VII. He acted as a mediator between Louis IV of France and the French princes who did not want to recognize him as king. He obtained the good result he hoped for. He had to put up with the obnoxious presence in Rome of Alberic who, heedless of the pontiff himself, oppressed the city. On the other hand Stephen owed it to him if he was elected pope. In those years Berengar II, marquis of Ivrea, was made king of Italy by acclamation.

128. MARINUS II (942-946)

Born in Rome, Marinus too governed the Church subjected to the will and interests of Alberic. But he was spiritual and full of humanity. His concern was to help the needy. And then, following the work of Leo VII, he dedicated himself to putting the monasteries in order which included intervening in their rules. During his papacy Hugh of Provence abdicated in favor of his son Lothair who was put under the tutelage of Berengar II, king of Italy.

129. AGAPITUS II (946-955)

Born in Rome, his election too was certainly the work of Alberic II whose position, however, had been seriously weakened. This enabled Agapitus to shake off a little of his importunate power. But if he was winning a certain independence from Alberic, there was a new peril on the horizon: the German princes under Otto I. Agapitus found himself involved, despite himself, in the murky business of imperial politics without being able to take action. Lothair, who was under the tutelage of Berengar II, died, possibly poisoned by the hand of Berengar himself. Berengar wanted to force Adelaide, the widow, to marry his own son. Adelaide gave a curt refusal and turned for help and protection to Otto I of Saxony. Otto married her and was crowned king of Italy. There was nothing for Berengar to do but submit to Otto. But he still got what he was after because Otto made him governor of Italy as his vassal. Thus Italy became a fief of the empire. In 954 Alberic II died, leaving the pope a liberated Rome which had only been waiting for good government. In those years, Harold, king of Denmark, converted to Christianity.

130. JOHN XII (955-964)

He was probably born in Rome of the counts of Tuscolo family. His name was Octavian and so he changed it. He was the son of Alberic II and was elected at the age of eighteen. In those years Bernegar ruled Italy by imperial command, but he had had to humble himself to obtain the charge. So he took hard vengeance on those feudal lords who had not supported him against the emperor. Pope John also took the consequences for having tried clumsily to enlarge St. Peter's territories at Berengar's expense. The latter began to make threats and the pope was quick to turn to Otto who came to Italy to put things into order. He obliged John to crown him emperor again and in effect restored the Holy Roman Empire. John had assumed obligations of fidelity towards Otto but he very soon began to ignore them and even made rapprochements with his old enemies Berengar and Lambert. Otto rushed back to Rome, this time with ugly intentions towards the pope. Taking advantage of the licentious life the latter led, Otto convened a council of bishops and had him deposed in favor of his own secretary Leo. He seized the occasion to take back a right which had been that of the Eastern emperor plus a not small addition: the election of the pope not only had to be sanctioned by the emperor, but the elected pope also had to swear an oath of fidelity to him. To win the support of the bishops, Otto gave them political power over the city as well and freed them from the authority of the princes, thus making them independent and giving birth to the institution of prince-bishops which for many years was a source of conflict between the Church and the Empire. John did not surrender. He fled Rome and returned with an army, then called a synod that deposed Leo who, in any case, had already fled to Otto's court and devoted himself to taking revenge on his enemies. Otto was obliged to come to Rome for a third time. But John died before he arrived. At only 27 years of age he died of apoplexy or, according to rumors, killed by an outraged husband.

131. LEO VIII (963-965)

Born in Rome, he was elected by the desire of Otto I in a council the latter called in Rome the same day on which the licentious John XII was deposed. For this reason some consider him to be an anti-pope. He was, in any case, totally subjected to the interests of the empire and his brief pontificate was turbulent.

In fact he first had to come to grips with John XII whose place he had taken, then with Benedict V whom the Roman people had elected after the death of John XII (964). He was unloved by the Romans, perhaps because he had been imposed by a foreign ruler. Among his few recorded acts is the excommunication he ordered for laymen who entered the presbytery during the Holy Office.

132. BENEDICT V (964-966)

Born in Rome, he was elected by the people after the death of John XII in opposition to Leo VIII who had been imposed by the Emperor Otto II. The emperor would not sanction his election and considered him to be an anti-pope. He had him imprisoned and transported to Germany. When Leo VIII died, Otto allowed him to return to Rome, giving in to the repeated demands of the Romans, the Franks and some of his subjects. But Benedict died in Hamburg with the reputation of a saint. It was to be Otto III to have his remains returned to Rome where he was buried in the Vatican Grottoes. It should be noted that both Leo and Benedict have been approved by the Church on the basis that their elections are valid under canon law.

133. JOHN XIII (965-972)

He was born in Rome of the Crescentius family, son of the Bishop John and Theodora II, sister of Marozia. He was elected directly after the death of Leo VIII but ten months before Benedict V died. He was imposed by Otto who continued to have his favorites elected in opposition to the Roman clergy who followed an independent line. John was not accepted by the Roman people.

Obliged to flee, he took refuge with Pandolf, prince of Capua and Benevento. From there he called on the emperor to intervene. The latter announced his imminent arrival in Italy. At this point the Romans recalled John. Those who had directed the rebellion against him were barabarously massacred by Otto's order. Among these was the Roman prefect Peter. The emperor stayed on in Rome for no less than six years, during which time he had the pope crown his son and successor Otto II. What is remembered of John is above all his pastoral zeal in fostering missions in Hungary and Poland. He protected monasticism and called various councils for the purpose of reordering and reorganizing the ecclesiastical structure.

134. BENEDICT VI (973-974)

Born in Rome, his was a brief and unfortunate pontificate despite his belonging to the party favoring Emperor Otto II who approved and supported him. But Otto's ascent to the throne had unleashed a strong reaction by the party opposed to the Germans with John Crescentius at its head. This latter left from Castel Sant'Angelo in a move against German positions. Benedict, of the imperial faction, did his best to calm things down, but it only got him cast into prison. He was freed once and then subsequently locked up in Castel Sant'Angelo by a certain Francone who had usurped the papacy giving himself the name of Boniface VII. But after a month he fled from fear of the Counts of Tuscolo who were notorious partisans of the emperor. Then Benedict got his rightful place back. Things got no better, however, only worse. The anti-German factions continued to fight, and among those who suffered the consequences was Benedict VI who was strangled and thrown into the Tiber only shortly before the imperial legate, Sicco, arrived in Rome to help him. His body was quickly fished out of the river and buried in the Vatican Grottoes.

135. BENEDICT VII (974-983)

Born in Rome of the Counts of Tuscolo family, he was thus pro-German. He led a pious, saintly life and was dynamic and energetic. Among his most salient acts was to call two councils in which Otto II also participated: one was called to excommunicate Franco who had usurped the papacy, while the second was to condemn simony. Meanwhile Otto II died at the age of only 28. His little son Otto III succeeded him (983). It was a favorable occasion for many disorders to erupt with death and violence of all kinds. The struggles were provoked by the nationalistic anti-German party still led by one of the Crescentius family. This party had two aims: liberate Italy from German rule and to reconstitute the Roman Republic. Benedict was buried in the Church of Santa Croce in Gerusalemme.

136. JOHN XIV (983-984)

Born in Pavia, his name was Peter Panecanova which he changed out of respect for the apostle Peter. Otto II had just died and chaos reigned in Rome. Franco took advantage of this to return from exile in Constantinople and seat himself on the papal throne once more with the same name of Boniface VII. He got rid of John by locking him up in Castel Sant'Angelo where he died in four months from hunger, abuse and, possibly, poison. His remains are interred in St. Peter's. Franco remained the master of Rome for almost a year after John's death when he too died (985), perhaps assassinated. The populace dragged his body through the streets, depositing it in front of St. John Lateran. Some priests gathered it up and buried it. But another story says his body was cut into pieces and thrown into the river Tiber.

137. JOHN XV (985-996)

Born in Rome, his election came a month after the death of the anti-pope Boniface VII and a year after the death of his legitimate predecessor John XIV. His pontificate was very long for those days, eleven years, probably because he had good relations with both the Crescentius family and the imperial court. Thus he could work in peace for the benefit of the Church. He sent the abbot Boniface to France to smooth out the conflicts that had arisen in the Church of Reims. Hugh Capet had asked him to do so. John was the first pope to emit a formal decree of canonization. He did so by elevating to sanctity Ulrich of the Counts of Dillingen. A defect is attributed to him, however: excessive concern with increasing the wealth and power of his own family. For this reason he attracted the dislike of the Romans.

138. GREGORY V (996-999)

Bruno of the dukes of Carinthia family was born in Saxony and became pope by desire of his cousin, Otto III. The emperor had entered Italy to quell the insurrections provoked by the national independence party headed by one of the Crescentius family. Otto managed one way or another to put a stop to the fight, Crescentius was pardoned and Otto returned to Germany. But the peace was of brief duration. Crescentius began acting up again in a way that forced the pope to flee to Pavia. An anti-pope was named in his place, John XVI (Philagathos). Otto came rushing back to Italy, reinstated Gregory as pope and had Crescentius beheaded. The Romans mourned this man they had esteemed and liked. The anti-pope was mutilated and locked up in a monastery where he died a few years later. Gregory died of malaria at the age of 27.

139. SILVESTER II (999-1003)

Born in France, he was the first French pope. His name was Gerbert and he was a Benedictine monk. Otto III nominated him, having had him as his tutor. Silvester's pontificate coincided with the passage from the first to the second millennium which the Christians considered to be a crucial time. Everyone expected the end of the world and prepared themselves for it with prayers, penitence and pilgrimages to the Holy Land. In agreement with the emperor he tried to reform and raise the morality of the clergy, but he did not get very far in this attempt. The progressive enrichment of all the ecclesiastical ranks and the growing phenomenon of prince-bishops had caused a great layicization and a noteworthy decline in the moral and religious level. Among other things the prince-bishops were subjects of the emperor first and foremost and only then bishops of the Church. The conflict experienced by these men in coming to grips with two contrasting powers generally ended with the victory of the temporal one to the disadvantage of the religious one. Thus the pope's reformist tendency was strongly opposed by the bishops. Meanwhile the independent nationalist party, which aimed at creating a Roman republic, had convened at Tivoli to oppose the papal authority, supported in this effort by several feudal lords. Otto came and put them down, but he died not long after and the pope lacked support in facing the dangerous situation. In the end, abandoning all attempts at reform Silvester limited himself to exclusively religious questions, induced into taking this attitude by the arrogance of Rome's new master John II Crescentius who made it his immediate business to get the pope under his thumb. Silvester may have died of malarial fever or possibly by assassination. Legend says Silvester was punished by God because he was an astrologer as well as a "necromancer and a sorcerer". Therefore his grave knows no proper repose but exudes a kind of sweat every time a pope is about to die.

140. JOHN XVII (1003-1003)

Born in Rome of a family called Seco or Secchi, his name was Siccone, he was married and had three children. He was elected by the desire of John II Crescentius. Of his very brief pontificate - six months - nothing important has been remembered. He was buried in St. John Lateran. With regard to the numeration XVII, it must be said that the same number was attributed to John Philagathos, the anti-pope nominated by Crescentius, while there had never been a John XVI. Some medieval chronicles apply the number XVIII to our Siccone which means that either the anti-pope Philagathos was considered legitimate, or else the historically fictitious John XVI was considered to have really existed. Furthermore, John XVIII is sometimes enumerated as XIX or even XX, one does not know why, and the error has come down almost to the present day. To arrive at complete clarity is an almost impossible task.

141. John XVIII (1004-1009)

Born in Rome, his name was Fasanus. For the numeration XVIII see the preceding entry. He crowned Henry II of Bavaria king of Italy. The ritual took place at Pavia. But the city rebelled, being sick and tired of the vexations caused by the German troops. So Henry conquered and sacked it. John did not intervene to prevent its destruction. He concerned himself with ironing out the conflicts between Rome and Constantinople, but without success. He was buried at St. Paul's outside the walls, having retired to its monastery where he ended his days as a monk.

142. SERGIUS IV (1009-1012)

Born in Rome, his name was Pietro Bocca di porco (Peter pig's mouth). Tradition says he was the first pope to change his name. This is not entirely true; others before him had changed theirs for various reasons. But it is true that after him all popes followed his example and changed their names on election except for the Dutchman Hadrian VI and Marcell II. He was elected thanks to the powerful support of the Crescentius family, but nevertheless he did not foster their interests. He was truly concerned with the good of the Church. The Italian princes were convinced by him to ally themselves against the Saracens in order to save the Holy Sepulchre from destruction. Sergius intervened authoritatively to resolve various problems and controversies between the Churche and the Empire. His constant concern was to raise the moral level and customs of the clergy, in particular bishops and abbots who were to involved in acquiring riches and power. He recognized St. Romuald's order of the Camaldoli. He was buried in St. John Lateran.

143. BENEDICT VIII (1012-1024)

Theophylact of the counts of Tuscolo was born in Rome. This powerful family was preparing to take the place of the Crescentius as the masters of Rome. The attempt of the latter family to impose their candidate, Gregory, did not succeed. Gregory was chased out and Benedict was able to seat himself on the papal throne also due to the strong support of Henry II whom he had gone to crown as emperor in Germany in the meantime.

During the twelve years of his papacy important things happened: the Saracens were defeated by the fleet that Benedict had armed with the help of Naples, Genoa and Pisa. The first Normans landed in Italy who, originating in Scandinavia, had just been in Jerusalem where they had defended the Holy Land. Coming from Normandy in France they established themselves in southern Italy and where henceforth always at the side of the Roman Church in the fight against the imperial power. Benedict convened a council in Pavia (1002) which emanated decrees for the reform of the clergy. In particular, it established that the clergy could not marry. Dispositions were also made against simony and duelling which was widely practiced at the time.

144. JOHN XIX (1024-1032)

A Roman of the counts of Tuscolo family, he was born in Rome and was the brother of Benedict VIII. He was a layman and received his sacred orders all at one time. To his brother Alberic he entrusted civil matters and reserved the religious ones for himself. Gifted with natural authority, he received respect and obedience from many of the powerful figures of his time. On the death of Henry II, John invited Conrad II to Rome and crowned him. The new emperor continued the policy of total support of the clergy initiated by his predecessor. This increased the power and authority of the bishops with respect to the lay vassals, but it also produced more disorders and conflicts. With Conrad's strong protection, John took a firm, intransigent position in questions regarding Constantinople and was able to govern the Church in relative tranquillity, fostering monasticism in particular. He gave his support to Guido of Arezzo, the famous inventor of musical notation. With regard to his number XIX, see John XVIII (140).

145. BENEDICT IX (1032-1044)

Theophylact of the counts of Tuscolo family was born in Rome and was a relative of Benedict VIII and John XIX. He was set on the papal throne at a very young age, some say as a child of twelve, imposed by his father Alberic who was the real master of Rome. His strange destiny led him to be elected three times and deposed twice. The first time he lasted twelve years. His licentious, deplorable life truly scandalized everyone. Nevertheless both the clergy and the people accepted him in order to keep peace and avoid bloodshed. But he was not accepted by the Crescentius family, the historical enemies of the counts. A merciless war broke out between the two families. Benedict called various synods: at Spello, Rome and Marseilles. Following a popular uprising led by the Crescentius family, Benedict was deposed for the first time and succeeded by Silvester III.

146. SILVESTER III (1045-1045)

His name was John and he was born in Rome. He was elected in place of Benedict IX and immediately deposed - fifty days after his election - through the intervention of the counts of Tuscolo who had brought their Benedict back to Rome. Silvester fled to the Sabine Hills where he continued to function as a bishop. To get him out of Rome they had to use force. His election was too obviously the fruit of political rather than ecclesiastical action, for which reason he should be considered an anti-pope. That, in fact, was the official judgement declared by the synod of Sutri in 1046. It is not known what he did for the rest of his life or how he ended it.

147. BENEDICT IX (1045-1045)

See no. 145. Benedict was returned to the papal throne by force which in the last analysis was his by right. But he only lasted twenty days after which he gave up the office to his cousin Gregory VI in exchange for a great deal of money. The whole situation accurately mirrors the life and mentality of the times: simony widely practised and accepted, a low level of morality, the ruthless use of power, force and overpowering aggression.

148. GREGORY VI (1045-1046)

John Gratian Pierleoni was born in Rome. He was a worthy and virtuous priest. Scandalized by the conduct of his cousin Benedict, he convinced him to abandon the papal throne in exchange for a large payment in money. After Benedict's retirement the people elected John Gratiano. The whole affair was conducted with the approval of the Roman clergy and so, one can say, in a good way to squelch the scandal and damage that Benedict had been causing as pope. Gregory immediately concerned himself with reforming customs and bringing order back to Rome. He was the one to create the first pontifical army for the purpose of liberating and defending the papal territories. But the story of money paid to buy the papacy disgusted Henry III. Calling on the privileges granted him by the *Privilegium Othonis*, he convened a council at Sutri (1046) which officially sanctioned the deposing of Benedict and the anti-pope Silvester III. The same council accepted the resignation Gregory gave of his own volition. He retired to the monastery of Cluny where he ended his life. Until his death he was assisted by Hildebrand of Soana, the future Gregory VIII.

149. CLEMENT II (1046-1047)

Suidger von Morsleben und Hornburg was born in Saxony. He was elected by the synod of Sutri which had at the same time deposed Benedict IX and the anti-pope Silvester III as well as accepting the resignation of Gregory VI. The synod had been convened by Henry III who had been disgusted by the disorders and immorality that accompanied the electing of popes and wanted to put an end to the scandalous situation by eliminating all others and elevating a worthy and valid person to the papacy. Thus he chose a priest he trusted of proven morality. The choice fell on Clement who was accepted by the Roman clergy and people. His first act was to crown Henry and the deposition that all papal nominations had to be made by the emperor. Thus the election again came under imperial control, but in compensation it was taken out of the hands of the nefarious Roman patrician families and the powerful feudal lords who were laymen aiming only to further their own material interests. He called a council that condemned simony. He followed Henry III to Germany, but on the return trip he was struck by a violent fever and died. He was buried in Bamberg in his homeland.

150. BENEDICT IX (1047-1048)

See numbers 145 and 147. On the death of Clement II, the counts of Tuscolo family brought their Benedict back to the papacy for the third time. But it was the last time fortunately for his own good and that of the Church. Following the sage advice of the saintly monk Bartholomew, the abbot of Grottaferrata (Rome), he definitively abdicated the papal throne and, penitent, retired to that monastery where he died and was buried.

151. DAMASUS II (1048)

Poppo of the Curagnoni family was born in Bavaria and was bishop of Brixen. He was indicated by Henry III of Germany after Aliard, bishop of Lyon, had refused. His very brief pontificate lasted only 23 days, dying of malarial fever in Palestrina. He is buried in the Roman basilica of San Lorenzo fuori le mura.

152. LEO IX, ST. (1949-1054)

Bruno of the counts of Egisheim-Dagsburg was born in Alsatia. He was a relative of Henry III who had him elected by a council of princes and bishops that met at Worms. Leo arrived in Rome and entered barefoot as a sign of humility accompanied by the duke of Lorraine and the monk Hildebrand whom he wanted by his side as a collaborator. Strong and energetic in character he performed his ministry with verve and courage. His objective was to bring morality back to a Church that was more and more the prey of simony and concubinage. Untiringly he crossed the length and breadth of Europe convening synods everywhere and calling everyone back to discipline and rectitude. To defend the Church he did not hesitate to make himself a warrior. In fact, he organized an army to fight the Normans who in southern Italy had taken territories away from the Church and who had abandoned themselves to sacking churches and monasteries. He confronted them in 1053 but was defeated and taken prisoner. To be liberated he had to make many concessions to them. But another and still greater sorrow was to be his before his death: during his pontificate the definitive break came between the Roman and Eastern Churches, the latter under the patriarch of Constantinople Michael Cerularius (1054). The major conflict regarded the supremacy of Rome over all the other churches which he did not want to recognize. The dissent and discord had already begun two centuries earlier (858). Leo died a short time after being freed by the Normans. He was buried in St. Peter's Basilica.

153. VICTOR II (1055-1057)

Gebhard of the counts of Dollnstein-Hirschberg was born in Bavaria. He too was a relative of Emperor Henry III and was his chancellor as Leo IX had been. He was elected a year after the death of his predecessor and was a very active pope. With the collaboration of Cardinal Hildebrand, who was one of his councillors, he began a vast reform and "cleaning up" of the institutions, the monasteries and the clergy, thus continuing the work of Leo IX. The aim was still the same: heal the sores of simony and concubinage. But he was not able to finish this job because of the strong resistance he met in the very circles he was trying to reform and because he died too soon. He tried to limit the emperor's influence in ecclesiastical affairs beginning with the election of the pope for which he demanded wide autonomy. He assisted Henry III in his death throes, having been asked to do so by little Henry IV who succeeded his father under the regency of his mother Agnes. Victor died suddenly of malarial fever in Arezzo and was buried at Ravenna.

154. STEPHEN IX (X) (1057-1058)

Originally called Frederick, he was born in Lorraine, a family member of the dukes of this region. He continued Victor II's work of moral regeneration by prohibiting the marriage of the clergy and between close relatives. He sent Cardinal Hildebrand of Soana to Germany to persuade Henry IV to cease trafficking in Church honors and posts. Power exchanges and simony were, in fact, common practice in Germany too. The strong resistance and difficulties he meat with made him lose heart and after a few months he abandoned the fight, retiring to the monastery at Montecassino. But he soon returned to Rome. Then Stephen left for Florence to discuss a plan for fighting the Normans with his brother Godfrey. There he was gripped by a violent malarial fever which killed him. The abbot Hugh of Cluny rushed to his bedside. Stephen made him and all the other cardinals present swear that they would elect no new pope before Hildebrand's return from Germany. He then died and was buried in the Florence Cathedral. Stephen's last wish was ignored. The Roman nobles would not wait and elected Pope John of Tuscolo who took the name of Benedict X. But he was not legitimately consecrated and so is considered an anti-pope.

155. NICHOLAS II (1059-1061)

Named Gerard, he was born at Chevron in French Burgundy. He was elected in Siena ten months after the death of Stephen IX where Hildebrandt convened the cardinals on his return from Germany. This election was in opposition to that held in Rome where the counts of Tuscolo had forcibly imposed one of their family, Benedict X. He was not recognized by the cardinals and so considered an anti-pope. Helped by Hildebrand and St. Peter Damian, Nicholas did not enter Rome until calling a council at Sutri where Benedict was deposed and defrocked. Benedict died around 1070. Nicholas continued the fight against the licentious life led by the most part of the clergy and against the greed for money and power which had become normal behavior. To this end he convened a synod in Rome which took several important decisions: prohibited was the assigning of all ecclesiastical in exchange for money (simony); priests were forbidden to take wives and those who had done so were ordered to leave them on pain of being defrocked; laymen were prohibited from investing bishops without papal authorization; it was decided that the pope could be elected only by cardinals without interference from the clergy, the feudal lords, the Roman populace and the emperor who only had the right of confirming the election. The reaction was violent and disobedience rife. In Germany they went so far as to call another council annulling the decisions taken in Rome. At that point, Nicholas realized that he needed a sure and loyal ally capable of protecting the Church from all kinds of disorder and from German interference. And it had to be an ally prepared to use the force of arms to "convince" the reluctant. He thought he had found his man in Robert Guiscard, the king of the Normans, who was the master of all southern Italy and who was only waiting to be officially legitimized. The pope gave it to him by granting him the title of vassal of the Church. Nicholas died in Florence where he is buried in the cathedral.

156. ALEXANDER II (1061-1073)

Anselm da Baggio was his name and he was born in Milan. He was elected at Terracina, having been designated by Cardinal Hildebrand. But the Emperor Henry IV would not confirm him since his rights had not been respected after having been abrogated at the synod in Rome called by Pope Nicholas II. By the order of the emperor another pope was elected in the person of Cadalus, the bishop of Parma, who took the name Honorius II. This latter reigned for eleven years, one year less than Alexander. The Church, of course, considered him an anti-pope, especially after a special synod of bishops was called in Mantua that accorded the papacy to Alexander. Many bloody riots ensued provoked by both parties. The Normans, keeping faith with the pact made with the Church, were always at its side and often intervened. Alexander called Henry IV to order various times but to no effect. On the other hand, he had good relations with the new English king, William, whom he blessed, and with the Spanish Church which had always been hostile towards Rome. He died after having governed the Church for more than eleven difficult and worrisome years.

157. GREGORY VII, ST. (1073-1085)

The omnipresent Hildebrand Aldobrandeschi was born of a humble family in Soana, Tuscany. With his great intelligence, energy and sharp political sense, he was the collaborator and councillor of no less than four popes. His enlightened and tireless work in favor of the Church was crowned in an almost natural way by his elevation to the papacy by popular acclamation during the funeral of Alexander II. The approval of the cardinals followed immediately. His first act was an attack on Emperor Henry IV who had presumed to ignore the decisions of the Synod of Rome and promulgated by Pope Nicholas II which regarded the papal elections and ecclesiastical morality and discipline. It will be remembered how on the election of Alexander II Henry had gone so far as to set up an opposing council and an anti-pope (Honorius II). Thus Gregory threatened to excommunicate anyone who opposed such decisions and decrees. Henry, who was an adult by now, accepted the challenge. He provoked an uprising in Rome led by one Cencio or Crescentius. The pope was seized as he was celebrating mass in Santa Maria Maggiore and locked up in a tower. The act was not only violent but sacrilegious. Immediately freed by the populace, Gregory called Henry to Rome to defend himself. But the only answer of the emperor was to call a council at Worms of bishops and make them declare the pope deposed, calling him "intrusive and illegitimate". The emperor had gone too far. Gregory called a council in Rome which approved and promulgated the famous *Dictatus papae* which is his masterpiece, a very clear and explicit synthesis of his conception of power. Power, both spiritual and temporal, is an emanation of divine power which operates in the world through the Church. The natural depository of this power is the head of the

Church, the Roman pontiff who is thus even above the emperor. It is the pope who authorizes the emperor to govern and not vice versa. Henry, who wanted to overturn divine law, was excommunicated. He was immediately abandoned by all of his subjects whom the pope had freed of their obligation of obedience and loyalty. The impression this made was enormous. There was little for Henry to do but go and reconcile himself with the pope. He was pardoned, but at a very high price. The happening at Canossa is very well known: Henry had to wait outside the castle for three days and three nights dressed in a cassock as a sign of penitence before the pope would receive him. This was tantamount to a humiliation. To have subjugated himself so totally may have rehabilitated him in Gregory's eyes, but it lost him much esteem in those of his feudal lords who before had urged him so intensely to effect a reconciliation. It was not a sufficient lesson for him, however, for once back in Germany he once again began hostilities against the pope who consequently excommunicated him a second time. This time Henry did not seek to have it revoked but decided to use force. He called a council at Magonza that deposed Gregory and set up an anti-pope against him, Clement III. Then he entered Italy and put siege to Rome which he conquered after three years. Actually it was the populace, tired of the siege, who opened the gates to him, forcing the pope to take refuge in the Castel Sant'Angelo. It was the faithful Robert Guiscard who saved Gregory by entering Rome and carrying the pope off to Salerno. There Gregory died and was buried.

158. VICTOR III, BL. (1086-1087)

Desiderius or Daufer was born at Montecassino of the princely *Epifani* family. He was a Benedictine monk and was expressly chosen by Gregory VII whom he had assisted as he lay dying. He was a meek man with mystical tendencies and ill suited to to manage a temporal power, particularly at a time of such difficulty for the papacy in open battle with Henry IV and the anti-pope Clement III. He was frightened by the legacy Gregory had left him. Therefore he thought of resigning. He retired to his beloved monastery of Montecassino. After a year he returned to Rome having finally decided to accept the office from a council which he himself had convened at Capua. As soon as he was ordained, Victor called another council, this time at Benevento, which confirmed the excommunication of Clement and made laws concerning ecclesiastical discipline. During his entire pontificate he was helped by the countess Mathilde and protected by Robert Guiscard. But Rome did not suit him and after a short time he returned to Montecassino where he died and was buried.

159. URBAN II, BL. (1088-1099)

He was born Odo de Lagèry near Reims in France. He could not come to Rome since Clement III still occupied the papal throne. His activities were inspired by his great predecessor Gregory VII, opposing Emperor Henry IV on the one hand and allying himself ever closer with the Normans on the other. He also laid the basis for a new relationship with the Byzantine emperor, *Alexis I Commenus* by accepting the latter's request for intervention against the infedels who were occupying the Holy Land. He renewed the excommunications for Henry IV and the anti-pope Clement against whom he continued to fight until Clement withdrew to Lombardy leaving Urban free rein. By now master of the situation, he was finally able to devote himself to the thing that history remembers him for:

the organizing of the First Crusade. There were various reasons for liberating the Holy Sepulchre and the Holy Land, not all of them religious in nature. The same request was insistently made by the French monk Pierre the Hermit whose preaching had already prepared the people for this event. Urban gave it the official blessing by calling a council at Clermont which declared war on the infidels and promised the remission of their sins to those who participated in the crusade. On the mentality of the times this promise had a potent effect. This First Crusade was the only successful one. The personages who took part in it passed into legend. Urban may not have learned of the victory because he died before the Christian army captured Jerusalem.

160. PASCHAL II (1099-1118)

He was born in Romagna at Bieda and called *Rainerius*. His pontificate was marked by a climate of confusion and agitation and the struggle against the German emperors which continued even more violently than before. The anti-pope Clement III who had been imposed by Henry IV took advantage of the empty chair to establish himself in Rome. Paschal called a council at the Lateran which renewed Henry IV's excommunication and decreed the expulsion of Clement which action was accomplished with the help of Roger of Sicily. Henry IV responded by naming a new anti-pope, Theoderic who was captured by Paschal and locked up in the Abbey of Cava where he soon died. Meanwhile Henry IV, dethroned by his own son Henry V, died in misery abandoned by everyone (1105). The new emperor proved to be the carbon copy of his father: he brought an army to Rome, took the pope prisoner and exiled him to the Sabine Hills. In his place he put a new antipope, Albert, who crowned him. But Albert too died soon and Henry wanted to attempt a reconciliation with Paschal. But the latter had gone to France to the court of Philipp I and so Henry decided to name another anti-pope, the fourth one, who was called Maginulfo and took the name of Silvester IV. But these nominations were only diversionary tactics for Henry who really wanted a reconciliation with Paschal and to resolve the serious discords, hopefully in his own favor, that made them antagonists. The point of contention was always the same: the right of investiture and which of the two powers had supremacy over the other. The two of them clashed repeatedly without ever reaching an agreement. In the end Paschal, exhausted by the long dispute, died and was buried in the Lateran. Paschal II concerned himself greatly with urbanism and ecclesiastical building, restoring many churches and building new ones. During his pontificate various knightly orders were created whose job was to protect the Holy Land and the pilgrims who travelled there: the famous Templars, the Teutonic Knights and the Knights Hospitallers.

161. GELASIUS II (1118-1119)

John Caetani, perhaps was born at Gaeta. For thirty years he held the post of chancellor of the Church. His pontificate was short and excruciating. As soon as he entered Rome he was attacked by Henry V's partisans led by Cencius Frangipane who seized him by the throat and beat him brutally while inviting others to give the same treatment to the cardinals who had elected him. Locked up in the tower of the Frangipanes, he was later freed by the people and so could return to Rome. But the sudden arrival of Henry V forced him to flee. He took refuge at Gaeta where he was able to be consecrated. Henry elected a new anti-pope - the fifth, no less! - Gregory VIII. From his seat in Gaeta Gelasius excommunicated both of them. Once the emperor had left for Germany, the pope returned to Rome. But he was chased out more by an uprising of the nobles led once again by Frangipane. Gelasius went to France to the court of Louis VI. He held a synod at Vienne and then retired to Cluny where he stayed until his death. He was laid in the bare earth dressed only in his monk's frock.

162. CALLISTUS II (1119-1124)

Guido of Burgundy was born in France and elected at Cluny where Gelasius II had died. He accepted with reservations, wanting first to know the opinion of the Roman cardinals and people. Their approval arrived. Thanks to his distinct political talent and the help of Lamberto of Fiagnano, the future Honorius II, the thorny question of the investitures was concluded. Agreement and peace were achieved with the Treaty of Worms in 1122. There it was established that the bishops would be elected by the clergy of the diocese and only then approved by the imperial legates. The sequence of the investitures was also to vary according to the place where they were held: in Germany first the investiture was to be made and after that the consecration as bishop; in Italy this order was reversed. The last important act of Callistus's pontificate was the calling of the first Lateran council at which the Second Crusade was proclaimed. With the help of the Normans, Callistus forced the anti-pope Gregory VIII to leave Rome and enter a monastery. Callistus died suddenly and was buried at the Lateran. A few months later Henry V also died at only 44 years of age.

163. HONORIUS II (1124-1130)

He was born *Lamberto Scannabecchi di Fiagnano* near Imola. The Frangipane family imposed his candidacy, the same people who had organized the attack on Gelasius II. The candidate of the Pierleoni family, Teobaldo Boccadipietra, was set up in opposition to him and took the name Celestine II. The two popes did not want to make war on each other and both expressed their willingness to renounce the office. So the nominations were submitted to the Sacred College which pronounced in favor of Honorius. He who had worked so hard at the Worms Concordat, negotiating on behalf of Callistus II, continued this policy which aimed at affirming the supremacy of the papacy over the empire. Another of his objectives was to form a league of Christian princes for the holy war. Meanwhile Henry V had died and in the fight for succession between *Lothair of Saxony* and *Conrad of Swabia*, Honorius took the part of the former. With Lothair there began relations of reciprocal trust and collaboration. Honorius was forced to confirm unwillingly Roger of Sicily's investiture as duke of Apulia and Calabria. In fact he feared the latter's determined and ruthless desire for expansion. He fought the Albigenses heresy, calling a council against it in Toulouse. The agitated Roman scene gave him much cause for suffering with the bloody turbulence of the struggles between the Pierleoni and Frangipane families for mastery of the city. A very ill Honorius finally retired to the monastery of San Gregorio al Celio where he died. He was buried in the Lateran Basilica.

164. INNOCENT II (1130-1143)

Gregorio Papareschi or Guidoni was his name and he was born in Rome. His nomination was the wish of the Frangipane family and was opposed by Anacletus II, the candidate of the Pierleonis. In effect Anacletus became the lord of Rome and Innocent had to flee to France. With the support of St. Bernard he returned to Italy, travelling the length and breadth of the country and calling councils against Anacletus everywhere he went. In the end he called on the help of Lothair of Saxony who had already been shown the favor of Honorius II as the successor to Henry V. Lothair accompanied him to Rome showing him much obeisance - kissing his foot and leading the mule on which Innocent was riding - thus publicly displaying his submission and vassalage. In exchange he was crowned emperor. The contest between Innocent and Anacletus lasted eight years, each of them being able to boast of some aspect of legitimacy. On the death of Anacletus a new anti-pope was elected, Victor IV of the counts of Tuscolo. But after barely two months he resigned. The road was finally clear for Innocent to perform his ministry freely. He convened two councils, one in Rome and the other in France. The first council condemned the anti-pope Anacletus and excommunicated Roger of Sicily for having usurped the sovereignty of the pope over Apulia and Calabria. To impose his rights the pope declared war on Roger but was taken prisoner along with his cardinals and obliged to sign a humiliating peace treaty. The second council, held at Sens, condemned the heresy of the philosopher Peter Abelard and excommunicated King Louis VII of France for showing sympathy to Abelard's doctrine. Innocent had the Church of Santa Maria in Trastevere restored and decorated with splendid mosaics.

165. CELESTINE II (1143-1144)

He was born *Guido di Castello* in Umbria and was papal legate to France under Honorius II. There he got to know Peter Abelard whose disciple he appears to have been, if only for a short time. For this reason St. Bernard criticized him harshly, especially for having maintained relations with the philosopher after Innocent II had condemned him. Once elected pope, however, he condemned the doctrine. He did not want to confirm Roger's investiture as king of Sicily and Apulia, but he withdrew the excommunication of Louis VII, king of France, when Louis asked his pardon. He made use of the collaboration of St. Bernard in the attempt to resolve the conflicts and controversies within the Church, but with meagre results. Those were the years when in which Arnold of Brescia was agitating souls with his vehement sermons against corruption and going as far as to contest the pope's authority. Intimidated by the overheated atmosphere, Celestine retired to a fortified monastery where he ended his days and his short pontificate.

166. LUCIUS II (1144-1145)

Gerardo Caccianemici was born in Bologna. His election went unopposed, but the situation in Rome was very serious. Rome was now going the way of other parts of Italy where the cities were affirming their independence and a freedom movement was openly contesting the power of the papacy. In the Church-State this opposition also took on a moral and religious character. The monk Arnold of Brescia was the spokesman of this malaise and this movement. He spoke vehemently against the temporal power of the popes and against the greed and licentiousness of the clergy. The malaise was real, evident and deeply rooted. In the Campidoglio a Roman Senate had established itself with a government headed by Giordano Pierleoni, the brother of the anti-pope Anacletus II. He *declared the temporal power of the popes to be abolished* and recognized only their spiritual power. Lucius fought the Pierleonis energetically and even moved some troops against them. During one of these war operations that besieged the Campidoglio, he was hit by a stone and died within a few days. In that year (1145) Alfonso I created the kingdom of Portugal which he had won from the Arabs, and put it under the protection of the Church, declaring himself its vassal. Lucius was buried in St. John Lateran.

167. EUGENE III, BL. (1145-1153)

Pietro Bernardo Paganelli was born in Pisa. He was a Cistercian monk and a disciple of Bernardo di Chiaravalle. Eugenio was kept from having any say in the civil administration of the city of Rome. So he began a long pilgrimage going from city to city until he eventually reached France where he held a couple of synods and a council. In Reims he managed to organize the start of the Second Crusade which had already been proposed by Callistus II. War on the Muslims was made and Louis VII of France as well as Conrad III of Germany joined in it, but the result was a clamorous failure. The indefatigable Bernardo di Chiaravalle, always faithfully at the pope's side promoted it. In 1152 Conrad III died and was succeeded by Frederick Harbarossa. Eugene made agreements with the new emperor: in the Treaty of Constance Frederick commited himself to defending the "honor of the Church" and the "patrimony of St. Peter", whereas the pope promised him a coronation and the "honor of the Empire". On the strength of that support Eugene was able to return to Rome, take possession of it and reach an agreement with the Romans. He was very hard on Arnaldo da Brescia, excommunicating him and chasing him out of the city. Eugene began construction of a "new palace" which is considered the original nucleus of today's Vatican palaces. He also completely restored Santa Maria Maggiore. He dictated the norms for the composition of the *Sacred College* which was officially established in 1150. He approved the Sovereign Military Order of Malta (the Knights of Malta). He died in Tivoli and is buried in the Vatican Grottoes.

168. ANASTASIUS IV (1153-1154)

Corrado "della Suburra", was named for a quarter of Rome where he was born of a noble family. He had been a supporter of Innocent II against the anti-pope Anacletus II. He was elected at an advanced age but by general consensus. It was a relatively peaceful time in which he governed the Church. He confirmed the Order of the Knights of Malta allowing them to accept donations from the faithful for the purpose of helping pilgrims to the Holy Land. He is remembered for the assistance he gave to the people during a famine. He was buried in the Lateran. An old tradition says that his remains were deposited in an urn that had belonged to St. Helen.

169. HADRIAN IV (1154-1159)

Nicholas Breakspear was born in London of a humble family. He was the only English pope in history. He would not accept the situation that had been created in Rome: a civilian government with a senate independent of the pope and Arnaldo da Brescia who continually hammered away at the people and instigating them. He launched an interdiction against the city until Arnaldo should be chased out. It was the first time such a thing had happened and the people were mightily impressed. The senate gave in and Arnaldo was sent away. Hadrian stopped at nothing to defend the supremacy of the Church over the Empire, thus challenging the Emperor Frederick Barbarossa. Nevertheless he accepted a meeting with him at Sutri. This is where the famous incident of the stirrups took place. Frederick did not want to hold the stirrups of the pope's horse and Hadrian refused to give him the kiss of pardon. The conflict was smoothed out on a diplomatic level and Frederick was crowned emperor. The one who had to pay for this was poor Arnaldo da Brescia who was captured, delivered to the pope and burned at the stake. Everything Hadrian did was based on the conviction that the Church was the central, unifying element of the Christian world and had as such to enjoy a privileged position above everyone and everything else. Barbarossa thought the exact opposite. Having restored the Empire's rights and control over all northern Italy, he also laid claim to the exclusive rights of the "Roman" emperors to Rome, thus seriously threatening the temporal power of the popes and the independence of the Pontifical State. The two personages drew further and further apart. Hadrian, given the untrustworthyness of Frederick, had a rapprochement with the Normans and signed the Concordat of Benevento with them. The break reached the point that Hadrian threatened to excommunicate Frederick. He did not have time to do so, however, because he died first.

170. ALEXANDER III (1159-1181)

He was born *Rolando Bandinelli* in Siena. Having a fighting spirit, he energetically opposed Frederick Barbarossa and his expansionistic plans. The emperor's partisans set an anti-pope up against him, Victor IV. Barbarossa convened the two of them, but since Alexander did not make an appearance, Victor was proclaimed pope and he settled down in Rome. For Alexander it was the beginning of a long period of suffering, conflict and travel that took him to various Italian and French cities in search of allies against Frederick. Hadrian lavished most of his energy on fighting him. After pronouncing excommunication on Frederick and Victor, Hadrian made a pact with the Venetians and the Normans and he joined the Lombard League. Meanwhile Victor died 1164. Barbarossa immediately named a new anti-pope, Paschal III, who held the office for four years before he too died. He was followed by Callistus III who, after a ten-year reign, subjected himself to Alexander of his own accord, obtaining a pardon and some rewards. What decided Callistus to subjugate himself were probably some political reasons: his protector Frederick had in fact begun to suffer some defeats and lose a great deal of power. In 1176 he was defeated at the battle of Legnano by the Lombard League. Frederick realized that the balance of power had changed and gave up the fight. He signed a treaty in which he renounced all imperial claims and recognizing Alexander as the one true pope. He had to accept some particularly humiliating conditions. It was the pontiff himself who raged pitilessly against him: as he put his foot on Frederick's bowed head he recited the biblical verses "Thou shalt crush the asp and the basilisk under foot". Alexander was finally able to enter Rome. Barbarossa, meanwhile had been humiliated but not tamed. He still had the power to support a fifth anti-pope, Innocent III, who however died after barely a year. Alexander had won and so could devote himself in peace to more strictly church business. He called and celebrated the Third Lateran Council during which 27 canons were approved. The most important of these was *Licet de vitanda* which decreed that the pope was to be elected only by the cardinals and with a two thirds majority of the votes. Another council held at Alby in France condemned the Albigenses sect which preached against several dogmas, against the authority of the pope and the corruption of the clergy. Alexander did not have an easy life even after Barbarossa's capitulation for there was still a strong pro-imperial faction in Rome that was against the pope. More than once he was forced to flee the city and take refuge elsewhere. He died victorious but exhausted at Civita Castellana and was buried in the Lateran.

171. LUCIUS III (1181-1185)

He was born *Ubaldo Allucignoli* in Lucca. Frederick Barbarossa held him in great esteem even while remaining faithful to Alexander III. After his election he stayed in Rome for only a few days. Due to the disorders that disturbed the city he was forced to leave and never returned. He settled in Verona and always remained in northern Italy. In Verona he met with Frederick Barbarossa, negotiating with him about several unresolved questions and asking for his help to return to Rome. The emperor refused and so Lucius would not crown his son Henry VI. Lucius III promulgated a constitution *Ad abolendam* which contained a group of norms for the repression of the many heresies that were flourishing. The constitution intended to be a rapid and efficacious instrument for pin-pointing and condemning all deviant forms of Catholic orthodoxy. It was the embryo from which grew the famous court of the Inquisition and of the Holy Office. The act of physically punishing heretics was entrusted to the "secular arm" which is to say the temporal power. One of the first heresies to pay the price was the Waldensian one. Lucius died at Verona and was buried in the cathedral there.

172. URBAN III (1185-1187)

He was born *Umberto Crivelli* in Milan. He was the archbishop of that city, an office which he kept even after being elected pope. He was elected by a conclave held in Verona which he made his seat since Rome was in chaos. Urban too had to confront harsh battles with Barbarossa who, after the death of the pugnacious Alexander III, had returned to an openly hostile attitude towards the papacy. Urban tried for a rapprochement with Frederick and urged an entente. He would have liked to resolve the outstanding problems left over by Lucius III: the inheritance of Matilda di Canossa and the Sicilian question. Thus he summoned the emperor to Verona, but the latter did not come. Added to this affront were two other things that increased the pope's resentment and the ensuing definitive break between the two powers: the marriage between Frederick Barabarossa's son and Constance, the daughter of Roger of Sicily. The popes had opposed this union as representing a danger for the Church which would have been caught as in a vice between North and South. The other thing was Henry's invasion of some papal territories. Thus Urban left for Venice where he intended to solemnly excommunicate Frederick. But he never arrived nor had time to pronounce the excommunication because of his sudden death at Ferrara in 1187. According to the chronicles he died of heart-break on receiving the news that Saladin had defeated the Christian army and had entered Jerusalem. He is buried in the Ferrara Cathedral.

173. GREGORY VIII (1187-1187)

He was born *Alberto di Morra* at Benevento and was elected at Ferrara. His pontificate was very short and entirely occupied with organizing the Third Crusade. Saladin had conquered Jerusalem in that very year and this was the Christian response. Death took him in Pisa where he was trying to pacify the Pisa-Genoa conflict and bring them together into the holy war against the Muslims. He tried to do the same with Frederick Barbarossa who the pope intended to be the cardinal point of the crusade, but the former persisted in his hostile attitude towards the Church. Thus the plan failed. He was buried in the Pisa Cathedral.

174. CLEMENT III (1187-1191)

He was born *Paolo Scolari* in Rome and was elected pope in Pisa where he was also consecrated. He had various friends in Rome who helped him smooth out relations with the senate. So he was able to return to Rome and given the republic's consent to stamp coins. He also made peace with Frederick Barbarossa who gave him back the territories that had been seized by Barbarossa's son Henry. Continuing the work of Gregory VII he organized the Third Crusade (1189) in which Barbarossa himself participated along with Philip Augustus, king of France, and Richard-the-lion-hearted, the English king. Venice, Pisa and Genoa took part. Despite all this the Christian forces were beaten. The only thing Clement obtained from Saladin was permission to visit the Holy Sepulchre. Barbarossa died during the crusade and Richard was made prisoner by Leopold, duke of Austria. He was only freed on payment of a hefty ransom.

175. CELESTINE III (1191-1198)

Giacinto Bobone was born in Rome to the family that would later call itself Orsini. As soon as he was elected - at the age of 85 - he crowned Henry VI as emperor to succeed Frederick Barbarossa who died during the Third Crusade, thus fulfilling a promise made by his predecessor Clement III. Henry was domineering and cruel for which reason he was nicknamed "the Cyclops". He invaded all of Italy without respect for anyone. He ripped Apulia and Sicily from the Normans who were the pope's vassals, thus offending the very man who had protected and crowned him. In fact he realized he had gone too far and tried to win over Celestine's favor by promising him to mount a crusade against the infidel. And the pope's alarm was entirely justified, not only because he knew Henry, but also because the annexation of southern Italy by the Empire left the papal state practically encircled. But Celestine let him do what he wanted without interfering. Henry died suddenly at only 32 years of age and the empire passed into the hands of his young son Frederick II under the regency of his mother Constance. Frederick was crowned as king of Sicily. Once established on the island he would make of it a renowned center of art and culture. Celestine concerned himself with making peace between the marine republics of Pisa and Genoa, without actually succeeding. He regulated some disciplinary aspects of monastic life and confirmed again the indissolubility of matrimony. By now a very old 92, he considered resigning the papacy in favor of Giovanni Colonna when death came for him on January 8, 1198. He was buried in the Basilica of St. John Lateran.

176. INNOCENT III (1198-1216)

Lotario of the counts of Segni was born at Gavignano in Latium. He was 38 when elected. Innocent was endowed with great intelligence as well as political savvy. Under him the papacy reached the apex of its prestige and power. He took the same theocratic stance as Gregory VII (see 157). His constant aim was to win acceptance for the supremacy of the papacy: the Church above all other powers because the only arbiter and sole holder of the power of God. This gave the Church the right and the duty to take action whenever and however it considered it to be opportune. In consequence of this, its decisions are without appeal, not only in religious but in political matters as well. In application of these principles, Innocent proclaimed Frederick II, whose tutor he was, the king of Sicily; at the same time the crown of emperor, which was

Frederick's by right of succession, he gave to Otto of Brunswick, thus avoiding the concentration of all political power in the hands of one man. Each of these personages aimed at having both kingdoms for himself. Otto, who of the two did not keep faith with his promise to renounce pretensions to the kingdom of Sicily, was in fact excommunicated. The weapon of excommunication and of interdiction was used by him on more than one occasion: in England King John was excommunicated for refusing to accept the pope's choice for archbishop of Canterbury; and in France it was used against Philip II for refusing to reinstate his wife; in Spain it was the turn of Alfonso IX for incest. He was always heeded. He proposed another crusade, the fourth, for which Venice provided the ships - no less than 480 vessels! But the expedition was a real disaster. Still Innocent would not give up and already began thinking of a fifth crusade. He blessed and encouraged St. Francis of Assisi even while never approving the order. Innocent charged the Dominicans, who were undergoing a great development in those years, with investigating into sins against the faith and giving them the *Court of the Holy Office* as a tool. The Albigenses heresy was their prime target. This sect was exterminated, above all in France, where the Dominicans acted in an exaggerated way that went beyond Innocent's mandate which was to fight, not to massacre, them. To crown all the reform activities of doctrine and discipline, Innocent convened a council, the Fourth Lateran one, where all the principle dogmas of faith were affirmed and the disciplinary norms established that are still valid today such as going to confession and taking communion at least once a year... However these many important undertakings did not keep him from concerning himself with works of charity in a zealous and generous way. He founded and maintained at his own expense the Holy Spirit Hospital. At times of famine he distributed thousands of food rations to the poor. His untiring work was only stopped by his premature death at 57 in Perugia where he died from an attack of malaria while on a trip to organize the Fifth Crusade. At first he was buried in the cathedral of that city, then his remains were transferred to the Basilica of St. John Lateran.

177. HONORIUS III (1216-1227)

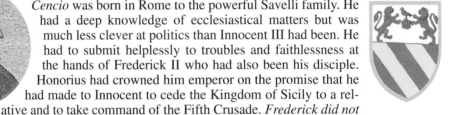

Cencio was born in Rome to the powerful Savelli family. He had a deep knowledge of ecclesiastical matters but was much less clever at politics than Innocent III had been. He had to submit helplessly to troubles and faithlessness at the hands of Frederick II who had also been his disciple. Honorius had crowned him emperor on the promise that he had made to Innocent to cede the Kingdom of Sicily to a relative and to take command of the Fifth Crusade. *Frederick did not keep his promises.* Honorius managed to launch the crusade without him, but this too came to an inglorious end. Honorius was more effective when dealing with religious matters and Church affairs. In particular he took great care of discipline and legal aspects regarding the election of popes and bishops by defending the rules and rituals. He ordered that the presbyters be better educated. He definitively approved the rules of the two new orders, Franciscan and Dominican, and confirmed that of the Carmelites. He left behind many writings, among them a life of Gregory VII, and died at a very advanced age. He was buried in Santa Maria Maggiore.

...GORY IX (1227-1241)

...was born at Anagni (Latium) to the counts of Segni, ...mily of Innocent III whose nephew he was. When ...d he was almost eighty years old. Gregory too had ... to suffer from Frederick II's arrogance and swag-...g, but he did it so tenaciously that Frederick had to ...rward to his death as a liberation. Gregory excom-...d him twice: once because Frederick, having left on ...ed back when the plague decimated his army (1227); ...cause he did not leave Sicily as he had promised to do. Frederick's ...n fact unleashed a series of bloody battles between the Guelphs and ...s the true reason for the excommunication. Gregory earned great ...rsity of Rome and for giving the University of Paris privileges and ...his name is linked to the institution of the Inquisition which he orga-...compiled the collections of the decrees of the last five popes into a ...*extra*. This was the nucleus of what would become under Pope Pius ... He dispensed the Franciscans from having to perform the normal ...y long and furnished them with a collection of prayers and rituals for ...n called a "breviary". He canonized Francis of Assisi, Anthony of ...man. He was almost 100 years old when he died.

179. CELESTINE IV (1241-1241)

Goffredo Castiglione was born in Milan. Gregory IX sent him to Montecassino to convince Frederick II to keep his famous promise to lead a crusade. He was the first pope to be elected by a true "conclave". It happened this way: when Gregory IX died the cardinals could not agree on whom to elect pope. The situation would not resolve itself and threatened to drag on endlessly. The senate and the people became impatient and took a historical initiative: they locked the cardinals up - *"cum clave"* - in the old Septizonium Palace on the Palatine Hill until they had elected someone. They remained there for several weeks in the heat and dreadful hygienic conditions with no one being allowed to enter or exit. Several of them became ill and one actually died. Celestine was elected in the end, already so old and ill that he died after only seventeen days.

180. INNOCENT IV (1243-1254)

He was born *Sinbaldo Fieschi* in Genoa. After two years of a vacant papal seat he was elected at Anagni where the cardinals had gathered to escape the pressures put on them in Rome. He began his papacy by breaking off relations with Frederick towards whom he took a hard, firm line. The struggle became heftier and Innocent had to flee Rome where the many partisans of the emperor were making things difficult for him. He went to Lyons in France where he called a council during which Frederick was declared a heretic, his excommunication confirmed, and his subjects released from their obligation to obey him. The emperor's reaction was violent. He unleashed open war against Innocent and began to strike at everyone who, in his opinion, took the part of the pope or merely sympathized with him. The fight ended only with the sudden death of Frederick in Apulia in the year 1250, possibly through betrayal. The only unresolved point around which the battle continued was the possession of Sicily which this time was claimed by Manfred,

Frederick's successor. But at this point Innocent returned to Italy. After a stay of two and a half years in Perugia during which he was present at the passing of St. Clare, he finally arrived back in Rome. Here he took several steps to restore order and the authority of the pope. One of these was the excommunication of *Ezzelino Romano*, the emperor's viceroy. He tried to make a pact with the nephew of Genghis Khan to have an ally in the war against the Turks and at the same time foster Christianity among the Tartars. During his pontificate, Louis IX of France left for the Seventh Crusade, but he was defeated and taken prisoner. Innocence died in Naples where he had gone to take care of several questions related to Frederick's succession. He was buried in the cathedral there.

181. ALEXANDER IV (1245-1261)

Rinaldo di Jenne was born at Segni (Latium). He was a relation of Gregory IX's who had made him a cardinal. He was a good and pious man but with so little bent for politics as to turn out weak and incapable. Nevertheless he followed the policies of his predecessors. He crowned Manfred king of Apulia and Sicily but demanded the right of vassalage for the Church. All the Norman kings had always promised this but never kept their promise. This time too no result was forthcoming so Manfred was excommunicated. Rome became an insecure place for the pope who fled to Viterbo. With no political abilities, Alexander applied his true talents and interests to Church affairs. He canonized St. Clare and decreed the stigmata of St. Francis to be genuine. He fostered the missions and urged the religious orders to follow their rules with greater rigor and fidelity. He wrote five books of decretals, a kind of popular jurisprudence. He prescribed a summary trial to combat heresies which were flourishing at that time. In particular, he fought against the flagellants who had become widespread in Perugia. He tried for a rapprochement with the Greek Church and a new crusade against the Turks without success. Alexander died in Viterbo and was buried in the cathedral there.

182. URBAN IV (1261-1264)

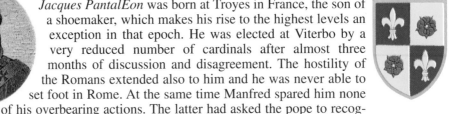

Jacques PantalÈon was born at Troyes in France, the son of a shoemaker, which makes his rise to the highest levels an exception in that epoch. He was elected at Viterbo by a very reduced number of cardinals after almost three months of discussion and disagreement. The hostility of the Romans extended also to him and he was never able to set foot in Rome. At the same time Manfred spared him none of his overbearing actions. The latter had asked the pope to recognize him as king of Sicily. When Urban refused, Manfred invaded the Pontifical State and threatened Rome itself. At that the pope excommunicated him and asked Louis IX of France for protection, offering him the Sicilian crown. He refused but suggested his brother Charles d'Anjou. After long negotiations Charles agreed to protect the Church in exchange for the crown of the Kingdom of Sicily. He swore fidelity to the pope and assumed the obligation to respect the status of vassal of the Church. Urban confirmed the pact and extended the holy day of Corpus Domini to the whole Church in honor of the famous miracle that had taken place at Bolsena (1247). Some time before he had modified the rules of the Inquisition. He died near Perugia and was buried there.

183 CLEMENT IV (1265-1268)

He was born *Guy Le Gros Foulque*, perhaps at Nimes, France. Before beginning his clerical career he was a soldier and then secretary to King Louis IX. He married and had two children. When he was left a widower he became a priest. He rose rapidly through the ranks of the clergy making many friends, among them St. Thomas Aquinas and St. Bonaventura. He was elected in Perugia by a conclave in which he was not present. Clement followed Urban's policy, allying himself with Charles d'Anjou against Manfred. According to the agreement made with Urban IV, Charles entered Italy and Clement crowned him in Naples. Then he attacked and defeated Manfred at Benevento. Manfred died in battle. He was succeeded by the very young Conradin who continued the fight but was defeated and taken prisoner. Ruthlessly cruel, Charles had him beheaded (1266) exciting the protests of the pope and general disdain and distress. Charles also kept his promise of conquering the kingdom of Apulia and Sicily as well as his obligations as a vassal of the Church. Clement was very pious, ascetic and rigorously moral: he ate no meat and went so far as to sleep on bare stone. He never showed favoritism to his relatives. He loved and fostered study, showing in this a humanistic spirit that was ahead of his times. With Louis IX he signed the "Pragmatic Sanction" which can be considered the first concordat regarding the relations of Church and State. He inspired the eighth and last crusade which was first led by Louis IX who died of plague in Tunis. Then it was Edward of England who carried on, the nephew of Richard-the-lion-hearted. But this crusade also failed. Clement died in Viterbo where he had always lived and was buried in the Dominican church there.

184. GREGORY X, BL. (1271-1276)

He was born *Tebaldo Visconti* at Piacenza. The famous conclave at Viterbo elected him, the longest in history, when an exasperated populace took the roof off the hall where the cardinals were holding their endless and fruitless negotiations. Divided into an Italian and a French faction, they could not decide on a nominee and three years had already passed since the death of Clement IV. Gregory had the reputation of a good, just and peace-loving man. At the time of his coronation he had to be ordained a priest and bishop. One of his first decisions as pope was to establish norms for the election of the pontiff: strict enclosure, gradual diminishing of food for the cardinals and the prohibition for them to use their own resources. He called a council at Lyon (1274) to discuss the following agenda: making peace with the Greek Church, liberating the Holy Land, raising moral standards. St. Thomas and St. Bonaventura were to participate, but the former died first and the second arrived late. *Flagellants* were once again condemned and the city of Florence put under *interdiction*. The two churches were reunited, if only briefly. The Eastern Emperor *Michael Palaeologus* was having problems with the Muslims and looked to Rome for military help. But once the danger was past everything returned as before. Even if power was not his aim, Gregory was responsible and clear-thinking. He considered it necessary to counterbalance the excessive power that Charles d'Anjou had won with something else. Thus he restored the German empire which had been without an emperor for about twenty years. He offered the imperial crown to Rudolf of Hapsburg who swore fidelity to him. The people loved Gregory and proclaimed him a saint. He died at Arezzo on his return from the council and was buried in the cathedral there.

185. INNOCENT V, BL. (1276-1276)

Pierre of Tarentaise or of Champigny was born at Moutier in France. He was a Dominican and a friend of St. Thomas Aquinus. His brief papacy still found time for some significant acts. He removed the interdiction from the city of Florence. He sought a rapprochement with Charles d'Anjou and reconfirmed his status as a Roman senator. He prohibited Rudolf of Habsburg from entering Italy before effecting a reconciliation with Charles d'Anjou. These decisions, apparently in conflict with those of his predecessor, had the precise aim of avoiding a bloody battle between the Guelphs and the Ghibellines. It is evident, however, that in some sense he was influenced by Charles and favored him over Rudolf. Innocent protected the religious orders and urged them to observe their rules strictly. His sanctity was recognized by the populace which called him "blessed". He died in Rome and was buried in the Lateran basilica.

186. Hadrian V (1276-1276)

He was born *Ottobono Fieschi* in Genoa to the powerful counts0 of Lavagna family. His relative Innocent IV had made him a cardinal. He had done a good job of his diplomatic work in England, Germany and Spain. He was elected even before having been ordained a priest. His papacy was so brief that he never even lived for his coronation. In fact, he had postponed his coronation to go to Viterbo for a cure since he was so old and ill. And there he died. It seems that he said to the cardinals around his bed: "I would rather that you had seen me as a healthy cardinal than a dying pope". It is known that he was a great miser. He is buried in the church of St. Francis in Viterbo inside a magnificent sarcaphogous sculpted by Arnolfo di Cambio.

187. JOHN XXI (1276-1277)

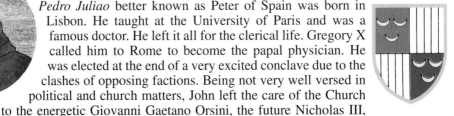

Pedro Juliao better known as Peter of Spain was born in Lisbon. He taught at the University of Paris and was a famous doctor. He left it all for the clerical life. Gregory X called him to Rome to become the papal physician. He was elected at the end of a very excited conclave due to the clashes of opposing factions. Being not very well versed in political and church matters, John left the care of the Church to the energetic Giovanni Gaetano Orsini, the future Nicholas III, and continued to occupy himself with his studies. His short pontificate had only one problem - finding the basis of an understanding between Charles d'Anjou and Rudolf of Hapsburg. But his efforts were in vain. He did have success obtaining a promise from Alfonso II of Aragon that the Portuguese Church would be respected and its revenues left to the clergy alone free of taxes and curtailments. He revoked the harsh disposition of Gregory X about keeping the cardinals cloistered in conclave. Old and ill, he retired to Viterbo, but the palace where he resided collapsed and John seems to have been a victim of it. He is buried in the cathedral there. His ordinal number "XXI" is sure to be an error, the effect of a mistake that goes back to John XIV (no. 136) who was counted twice. Furthermore there was never a pope with the number "XX" (it has been attributed to Romano of the counts of Tuscolo - no. 144 - who is sometimes indicated as John XIX and sometimes John XX) which means that by rights Peter of Spain should be called John XIX.

188. NICHOLAS III (1277-1280)

He was born *Giovanni Gaetano Orsini* in Rome. The conclave that elected him was held in Viterbo and lasted almost six months. He fixed his seat in the Vatican and lived there most of the time. For that purpose he had the so-called "little palace" of Nicholas III built which was the early nucleus of the Vatican buildings. A pope with a strong personality, he tried to balance the two forces that contended for Italy: he took away the vicariate of Tuscany from Charles d'Anjou and no longer elected him a Roman senator, while making Rudolf of Hapsburg recognize the Church's sovereignty over the Marches and Romagna. He continued the work of rapprochement with the Eastern Church already begun by John XXI, a project in which he displayed great tact and balance, particularly in ordering that the traditions and customs of the peoples of those parts. He protected the Franciscan and Dominican orders and concerned himself with missionary work sending priests as far as Mongolia. Nepotistic and miserly, he greatly favored his family. One need only consider that of the nine cardinals he nominated, three were his relatives. Besides the Vatican palace and gardens he built the church of S. Maria sopra Minerva, the famous Passetto di Borgo and the papal chapel, *Sancta Sanctorum*, at the top of the Holy Steps, full of beautiful mosaics. He died in Viterbo.

189. MARTIN IV (1277-1280)

Simon de Brion was born in France at Montpintiè. He was elected in Viterbo after six months of fighting and was practically forced on the conclave by Charles d'Anjou who happened to be in the city. Martin accepted reluctantly after much soul-searching. The ordinal number "IV" should actually be "II" because popes Marinus II (108) and III (128) were confused with Martin II and III. Once elected pope his policies were all in favor of Charles who as a personal friend had complete influence over him. Martin reelected Charles as Roman senator and gave the highest Church offices to French compatriots. During his pontificate the fierce and bloody rebellion against the French in Sicily erupted which is known as "the Sicilian Vespers". The news of the revolt in Palermo reached Rome where Charles was already unloved. The populace deposed him as senator and elected another in his place. Martin, being entirely on the side of Charles, excommunicated all those who were against his friend: the Palermo insurgents, Peter of Aragon, who had been elected king of Sicily in Charles's place and the Eastern Emperor Michael VIII guilty of having opposed Charles's attempt to take over the Latin empire of the East. When Charles died Martin had to flee Rome where his life was in danger. He went from city to city and settled in Perugia where he died. He was buried in the cathedral there. Dante consigns him to purgatory as a glutton because he had a great appetite for vernaccia wine and Lake Bolsena eels.

190. HONORIUS IV (1285-1287)

Giacomo Savelli was born in Rome and elected pope either in Viterbo or Perugia when he was 75 years old. As soon as he took possession of the papacy he nominated his brother Pandolfo a Roman senator, he too very old, half paralyzed and unable to move as was the pope himself due to a serious form of arthritis. In this way all power, civil and religious, was firmly in the hands of the Savelli. Otherwise Honorius was an honest and energetic man. He brought peace and benefited Rome by methods which were at times extreme but effective: he had ruffians and delinquents hanged and reduced the arrogant nobility to impotence. He also took action in Sicily where he had jurisdiction and made laws imposing peace and order. For the rest he was on the side of the Angevins, would not recognize Peter of Aragon as king of Sicily and excommunicated his wife Constance and his son James. He also used the weapon of excommunication against those in Viterbo who had interfered in the conclave which had elected Martin IV - they had broken into the hall and kidnapped two cardinals. He condemned the apostolic and flagellant sects along with all other non-orthdox religious associations. He introduced at the University of Paris the study of oriental languages for the instruction of missionaries to be sent to those lands. Honorius died on the Aventine Hill in the Church of Santa Sabina and his remains now rest in the Church of Aracoeli.

191. NICHOLAS IV (1288-1292)

Girolamo Masci was born at Ascoli Piceno. He was the general of the Franciscan order. After the death of Honorius IV the papacy was vacant for almost a year due to the disagreements among the cardinals and because a plague epidemic had struck Rome. As many as six cardinals had died and others had been taken ill. The conclave was suspended and the cardinals left the city. Only cardinal Masci stayed on and courageously concerned himself with purifying the environment by keeping many stoves lit all summer. With the coming of winter the plague ended, the Sacred College was able to meet again and it elected Nicholas. The Romans loved him and welcomed his election joyously. But after two years the political climate in Rome had become incandescent. The Colonnas and the Orsinis were at each others' throats and Nicholas made the mistake of taking the side of the former conferring on one of the family the office of single senator. He was obliged to flee Rome and took refuge at Rieti. His attempt to organize a new crusade to the Holy Land failed, but he had more success with the missionary work he promoted among the Mongols and Tartars. He established that half of the income of the Church go to the cardinals. He is remembered for the mosaics he had created in the basilicas of St. John Lateran and Santa Maria Maggiore. He also began construction on the cathedral of Orvieto.

192. CELESTINE V, ST. (1294-1294)

Pietro del Murrone was born at Isernia. He was of the Angeleri family but is known as Murrone because of the mountain to which he withdrew to live a hermit's life. The conclave that elected him lasted for two years and changed venue four times. Rome, Viterbo, Rieti and, finally, Perugia. divided as they were among the interests of the Colonnas and the Orsinis, the cardinals could not reach an agreement. The annoying length of the conclave irritated even such a man as Celestine who wrote a sorrowful letter to the cardinals urging them to decide. They then elected him, the saintly hermit, who had chosen a life contrary to the one to which he now was called. At first he refused the nomination, but in the end he accepted reluctantly considering it to be an act of obedience to God. Another reason undoubtedly motivated him: the hope of being able to reform and renew the Church in an evangelical direction. He was crowned at L'Aquila and made Naples his seat in the territory of the Angevins who immediately tried to bend him to their interests. All the projects he had dreamed of when elected were systematically opposed and frustrated by precisely the ecclesiastical hierarchy that ought to have helped him. His suffering and disappointment were so great that he gradually decided to resign from the papacy. He announced this decision in a papal bull where he affirmed the right of the pope to resign from the pontificate. According to some sources Celestine was forced to resign. The man who induced him to this drastic move would have been the astute and capable Cardinal Caetani, the future Boniface VII, a great jurist, to whom the pope had appealed for advice. As soon as he had renounced the papal tiara Celestine was led away and locked up, practically a prisoner, in the castle of Fumone under very hard and uncomfortable conditions. The total isolation imposed on him by Boniface VIII had the purpose, among others, of keeping his many disciples away - he had founded the order of the Celestines - who might have convinced him to change his mind. After a year and a half of imprisonment he died, possibly from violence. After only twenty years he was canonized at Avignon by Clement V (1313). His remains rest at L'Aquila in the church of Collemaggio.

193. Boniface VIII (1294-1303)

Benedetto Caetani was born at Agnani (Latium). He was energetic and decisive with great political talents that were made more effective by a remarkable culture and thorough juridical knowledge. He was elected at Naples in a very short conclave following Celestine's resignation which, according to some, was his doing. The large majority that elected him has made some people suspect corruption or even simony. But this would not seem to be the case if one considers his intransigence towards everyone as soon as he established himself in Rome to which he immediately returned the papal seat. He quickly brought the city to order, throttling each abuse and without regard for anyone, not even those who had supported him. Boniface was a convinced believer in the supremacy of spiritual power over all other power. In this sense he can be considered the third outstanding figure after Gregory VII and Innocent III in that "theocratic" line which despite its ups and downs, the dominant theme of all papal politics in the Middle Ages. It worked out the theory promulgated in various official documents and imposed by every possible means not excluding war and excommunication to the various exponents of political power in turn. Its illustrious victims were Henry IV, Frederick Barbarossa, Frederick II of Swabia and Philip IV of France. The relations of Boniface VIII with France alternated and were often contradictory. They are always to be interpreted in the light of his principle objective: affirm the supremacy of the Church and defend its interests, the material ones included. Consequently Boniface approached and distanced himself from France according to the situation and concerned most of all not to give to much room to the power of Philip IV. With the latter he engaged in a hard battle composed of fatherly admonitions, harshness of character, excommunications and pardons. He always confronted him with courage, unconcerned with the consequences he predictably had to face in his own person given the character and arrogance of Philip. One only need consider the aggression, unheard of against a pope, he was subjected to by Philip de Nogaret and Sciarra Colonna, Philip's emissaries and the infamous "slap" he received from the two of them when he was already old and dressed in sacred vestments. As is well known, Dante assigned him a place in hell while he was still alive, thus expressing his judgement and that of many of Boniface's adversaries on the pope's attitudes and politics. But the name of Boniface is remembered for the calling of the first jubilee in the history of the Church (1300) and the great "pardon" the pope accorded to all. His intention was clearly to show that the Church had and exercised a power above all others: that of pardoning all guilt and of opening the gates of paradise. This was the essence of the Church: its spiritual and redemptory function. This was perhaps Boniface's most profound message. To him is also attributed the foundation of Rome's "La Sapienza" University. To the pontifical coat-of-arms he added the papal tiara with a second crown superimposed representing royal power. The tiara, of which Paschal II (1099) had already spoken, is the symbol of spiritual power. Boniface died a short time after the sacrilegious slap.

194. BENEDICT XI, BL. (1303-1304)

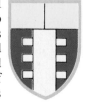

He was born *Niccolò Boccasini* at Treviso. Boniface III made him a cardinal and gave him many important jobs to carry out. NiccolÚ was with him when Benedict was humiliated at Agnani. He should have been numbered "X", but he refused the number because it had been used by an anti-pope (in 1058). Unlike his predecessor he was of humble and conciliatory temper. He pardoned the Colonnas and made a rapprochement with Philip IV. He partially rehabilitated the two Colonna cardinals whom Boniface VIII had excommunicated and exiled, but he was inflexible with Sciarra Colonna and Philip di Nogaret of the famous slap given to Christ's vicar. He tried unsuccessfully to arrange a peace between the Florentine Whites and Blacks. He died suddenly in Perugia after eating a plate of dried figs, possibly poisoned according to a common story of the time. He was buried there in the church of San Domenico.

195. CLEMENT V (1305-1314)

Born *Bertrand de Got* at Villandraut in France, Clement was elected at Perugia in a conclave that lasted fifteen months as a compromise nominee between the Italian cardinals and Philip IV. He was crowned at Lyons. During the ceremony Philip held the reins of the pope's horse for a moment in homage to his regal authority. But it was only a formality: Clement was always obliged to obey Philip. Pressed by the latter, Clement disowned the work and documents of Boniface VIII with the clear intention of damaging his memory. The same intention must be read into the canonization of Celestine V, done and proclaimed in a blazing hurry. Again on Philip's demand he abolished the order of the Knights Templar, the possessors of enormous wealth that Philip wanted to get his hands on. Its members were unjustly accused and many of them barbarously executed. Clement founded the universities of Perugia, Oxford and Orleans. He had great esteem for Giotto whom he took with him to Avignon. Inside the Avignon Cathedral, beside the central nave, he had a small chapel built which he used for his functions. Clement died at Bordeaux and is buried at Uzes.

196. JOHN XXII (1316-1334)

Jacques Duëze was born at Cahors, France. He was elected after two tormented years with the seat vacant. His number should be "XX" (see popes nos. 136 and 187). Despite bodily miseries, his mind was energetic and vital, and he led a pious, honest life. He excommunicated Ludwig of Bavaria, Henry VII's successor who had proclaimed himself emperor and held his coronation in Milan and Rome without the pope's approval. It was he who moved the papal seat permanently to Avignon and had built the large, grandiose palace that still stands there today. He led an intense ecclesiastical life, concerning himself with the controversial and thorny problem of Franciscan poverty which was being promoted with fanatical zeal by the so-called Franciscan Spirituals. Not succeeding by means of normal discussion, he was forced to fall back on his authority: he dispersed the most intransigent groups and put the most turbulent ones on trial. Many went to ask Ludwig of Bavaria for protection. He reaffirmed the principle that only the pope could nominate bishops. He introduced the Corpus Domini procession and the Most Holy Trinity holiday. He prescribed the daily reading of the Angelus at sunset in honor of the Blessed Virgin. He canonized St. Thomas Aquinas and established the court called the Sacra Rota because of the round shape of the table at which the judges sat. He sent missionaries to the Tartars and to Ceylon and he opposed magicians and alchemists. Towards the end he thought more and more often of returning to Rome. Almost ninety when he died, he was buried in the Avignon Cathedral.

197. BENEDICT XII (1334-1342)

Jacques Fournier was born in Toulouse. Once he became pope, he tried seriously to return the papal seat to Rome, or at least to Italy. Philip VI of Valois stopped him. Nevertheless he managed to have a say in Roman affairs and induced the Colonnas and Orsinis to live in peace together, at least for a while. Obliged to stay in Avignon, Benedict finished work on the palace begun by John XXII and devoted his attention to healing the corrupt uses and abuses at the papal court overflowing with prelates and bishops. Thus he abolished every kind of favoritism and obliged the bishops to go home and live in their own dioceses. He was upright and pious, sincerely concerned with Church affairs but absolutely lacking in political savvy. Therefore he had no idea about how to oppose the excommunicated Ludwig of Bavaria who published the Pragmatic Sanction in Frankfurt in which it was affirmed that the imperial rank was bestowed directly by God and had no need to be legitimized by the pope's consent. One will recall that Ludwig had proclaimed himself emperor without asking for the pope's confirmation and was therefore excommunicated by John XXII. With his policy of rigor and economy he managed to accumulate a veritable treasure. Benedict died at Avignon after a long illness and is buried there.

198. CLEMENT VI (1342-1352)

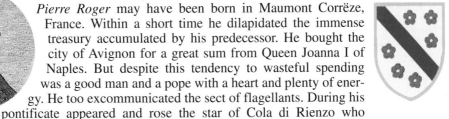

Pierre Roger may have been born in Maumont Corrëze, France. Within a short time he dilapidated the immense treasury accumulated by his predecessor. He bought the city of Avignon for a great sum from Queen Joanna I of Naples. But despite this tendency to wasteful spending was a good man and a pope with a heart and plenty of energy. He too excommunicated the sect of flagellants. During his pontificate appeared and rose the star of Cola di Rienzo who founded a republic in Rome with the pope absent. At first Clement lent him his support because he saw in him a valid tool for creating order and justice in the turbulence of Rome plagued by the bloody feud between the Colonna and Orsini families. He had shown courage and even-handedness and the Romans had given him dictatorial powers. He proclaimed himself "the tribune of freedom" and he did indeed pacify the city with wise and fair laws. But afterwards he went over to a regime of excesses and arrogance which tired the patience of the people and the patricians to the point of rebelling. Cola di Rienzo had to flee Rome but was caught and sent to the pope in Avignon who excommunicated him and kept him under constant surveillance. Clement pronounced an anathema against Ludwig of Bavaria and gave his support to King Charles IV of Bohemia, his friend and disciple. He gave custody of the sacred sites in the Holy Land to the Minorite monks and determined that Holy Year should be held every fifty years and not every hundred years as Boniface VIII had established. Clement called the Holy Year of 1350 but did not go to Rome for it. He died in Avignon and was buried at La Chaise-Dieu.

199. INNOCENT VI (1352-1362)

He was born *Etienne Aubert* at Monts Beyssac, Limousin, France. He was determined to reassert pontifical authority over the Papal State and to this purpose sent a papal legate to Rome - the energetic Cardinal Albornoz, an old aide of Cola di Rienzo with many friends and followers remaining in the city. The pope hoped that Cola, made tamer by imprisonment, could be restored to power and contribute to pacifying the ever more over-heated and turbulent situation in Rome. Cola was named governor but became more tyrannical than ever. This time the outraged populace, ably maneuvered by the Colonna family, killed him at the foot of the Campidoglio and tore his body to pieces. Albornoz continued with his job appointing another governor and with his astute policy obtained some good results. With regard to disciplinary matters within the Church, Innocent followed in the footsteps of Benedict XII: he was severe with the clergy demanding honesty and dedication from them. He instituted a system of examinations and merit for assigning ecclesiastical benefits and rewards. He once again obliged bishops to reside in their dioceses. More than once he attempted to smooth out the quarrels between England and France as well as fostering rapprochement with the Greek Church. But the results were meagre. Innocent died at Avignon, was buried there and given a monumental tomb.

200. URBAN V, BL. (1362-1370)

Guillaume de Grimoard was born at Grisac in France. He was a Benedictine monk and elected at Avignon. As pope he continued to live the austere and saintly life he had led as a monk. He concerned himself with ecclesiastical reform and the fostering of study by favoring the universities. He heeded the call coming from many parts and decided to return to Rome. In October 1367, on board a Venetian galley and accompanied by many Italian lords, he made the voyage to Rome where the populace received him triumphally. He tried to bring order to government and discipline to the clergy, eliminating abuses and privilege. But the task turned out to be extremely difficult because the customs were so degraded and the bad habits so ingrained. The situation was all the more precarious due to the raging of some companies of adventurers in the district who ruthlessly pillaged and killed. A discouraged and frightened Urban returned to Avignon, also because of a new outbreak in the Anglo-French conflict. St. Bridget of Sweden urged him to stay on (1370). Not even her gloomy prophecy of his death could make him change his mind. The prophecy was punctually fulfilled. As soon as he arrived in Avignon in fact, Urban died dressed in his monk's habit and laid out on a poor, austere mat. During his time in Rome he had many churches restored and rebuilt the monastery of Montecassino. He had the skulls of St. Peter and St. Paul brought to the Lateran basilica and installing them within the new tabernacle he had had built. He is the one to have added the third crown, or third order to the papal tiara, symbolizing temporal power. For this reason the papal headdress is also called "triregnum". Urban is buried in Marseille. Pope Pius IX beatified him.

201. GREGORY XI (1371-1378)

He was born Pierre Roger de Beaufort, possibly at Maumont in France. A relative of Clement VI, the latter made him a cardinal when he was only eighteen. As soon as he was elected he chased away all those bishops and prelates who had abandoned their dioceses and were living like established courtiers neglecting their pastoral duties. He ordered their immediate return home and to their work. But the thing for which history remembers him is having returned the seat of the papacy definitively to Rome after seventy years in Avignon. Many urgent calls induced him to this move, including some from St. Bridget of Sweden and St. Catherine of Siena. There was also the particular situation that had been created in Italy and Rome. The territories of the Papal State were in full rebellion. If the pope wanted to get control of the situation and keep the state united, he had to go to Rome and resume exercising power. This he did, overcoming the resistance of the French cardinals and bishops. In January 1377 Gregory entered Rome and established himself in the Vatican beside the tomb of St. Peter. One should remember that before the move to Avignon the popes resided at San Giovanni in Laterano. He died a year after his return to Rome at the age of only 47, exhausted and stricken by the continuous rebellions and plots going on around him. He was buried in the church of Santa Francesca Romana near the forum. He was the last French pope.

202. URBAN VI (1378-1389)

He was born Bartolomeo Prignano in Naples. The Sacred College, composed mainly of French cardinals, had to give heed to the explicit desire of the Roman populace who wanted a Roman, or, at least, an Italian pope. Urban was chosen because, even if Italian, he was also a subject of the Angevins, and thus acceptable to the French. But this acceptability was of short duration due to the dreadful character of the pope (they referred to him as "Inurbano VI" [meaning "rude"]) who was absolutely unbearable and lacking in all diplomacy. The very ones to have elected him set up an anti-pope in opposition in the person of Robert of Geneva who took the name of Clement VII. Urban sent troops against him and forced him to flee to Avignon where he was consecrated and established his seat. Thus began the schism lasting forty years that divided the Church between the partisans of the Roman pope and those of the one in Avignon. This was considered a great scandal by the faithful who saw their pastors fight shamelessly for a power that had become entirely secular and based on material interests. Partisans of the pope of Rome were Italy, Germany, England, Poland and Hungary; the pope of Avignon was supported by France, Spain, Portugal and the other parts of Europe. Urban called a Holy Year for 1390, but he did not live to see it having died the year before. No one at all wept for him with all the enemies and dislike he had created. The anti-pope Clement outlived him, dying in 1394.

203. BONIFACE IX (1389-1404)

He was born Pietro Tomacelli in Naples and was elected at only 34 years of age. Courteous and kind, unlike Urban VI, he tried to find a solution to the shameful condition of the Church by urging an understanding with the anti-pope Clement VII. He also tried to involve the French King Charles VI without success. Meanwhile Clement died and in his place was put the Spanish Pedro de Luna who took the name Benedict XIII. This anti-pope showed himself to be even more hostile than his predecessor and just as certain of his legitimacy. Therefore he refused any and all offers of negotiation, mediation and conciliation presented by Rome. Boniface called the Holy Year of 1400 which attracted so many pilgrims as to bring on a plague epidemic that spread like wildfire. During the Holy Year there arose in Provence the "White Sect", a kind of confraternity whose men and women dressed in white cloaks and hoods and flooded the squares flagellating themselves and crying "Peace and mercy". Despite the great pacification of the Holy Year the quarrel between Rome and Avignon continued, even worsened. One must attribute to Boniface behavior that was at least questionable: he used ecclesiastical indulgences and benefits to get the large sums of money he needed, establishing very high tariffs and paying no heed to the character of the people to whom they were being granted. Among Boniface's works there was the restoration of the Castel Sant'Angelo in Rome and the founding of the University of Ferrara. He was not loved by the people who rebelled on two occasions. He died at 45 and was buried in St. Peter's.

204. INNOCENT VII (1404-1406)

He was born Cosimo Migliorati in Sulmona, Abruzzo. He had vowed to refuse if he were nominated. But when it happened he accepted and was crowned. During the conclave he had made efforts to reach an agreement with Benedict XIII, but he never tried to really reach an understanding with him. On the contrary, he was entirely intransigent. Rather he undertook to pacify the feud between the two powerful Roman families the Colonnas and the Savellis so that the city could have some peace. In the course of an audience he granted to sixteen representatives of the people who were beginning to make threatening noises, a relative of the pope's killed eleven of them and threw their bodies into the street. The people rose up and obliged the pope to flee to Viterbo at night with all of his court. He could not return to Rome until the following year. Innocent was enamoured of study. He restructured the University of Rome introducing the new departments of medicine, philosophy and Greek. He died only a few months after returning to Rome.

205. GREGORY XII (1406-1415)

Angelo Correr was born in Venice and was eighty years old when elected. He had committed himself to renouncing the papacy if Benedict XIII would do the same who was still in his seat in Avignon. The anti-pope had made the same promise, but neither of them kept it. Then the Sacred College meeting in Pisa decided to bring an end to the dispute by deposing both and electing a new pope, Pietro Filargo, who took the name of Alexander V. Thus there were three popes all at once, each of them claiming legitimacy. Alexander V died very soon (1410). In his place Baldassare Cossa was elected who called himself John XXIII. This state of affairs of three simultaneous popes lasted from 1409 to 1417, the year of the end of the Council of Constance where the Pisa decision was confirmed. All three popes were thrown out and another, Martin V was imposed. Gregory XII was the only one to accept the decision. Benedict XIII continued to consider himself pope until his dying breath. John XXIII, considered dangerous, was imprisoned and kept segregated in various German castles from which, however, he managed to escape. He asked the new pope Martin for protection and it was accorded him even to the extent of giving him a place in the Sacred College on a chair higher than the others. He died soon afterwards. Gregory XII retired to Recanati after his resignation and died in 1417. He is buried in the cathedral there.

206. MARTIN V (1417-1431)

He was born Oddone Colonna in Genazzano (Latium) in 1368. He was one of the promoters of the council of Pisa and participated in the one at Constance which elected him. His election coincided with the deposiotion of the three other popes that had preceded him: Gregory XII, who is considered legitimate, Benedict XIII and John XXIII who are considered anti-popes. So, elected in 1417 he managed to enter Rome in 1420 after three years of roaming. The people greeted his entrance triumphally. In many years he was the first Roman pope. But his was not an easy papacy: he had to resolve several important problems. The first was a question of doctrine, namely, if councils were superior to popes. During the Council of Constance he had held that position. But once becoming pope he changed his mind: the pope was the supreme authority and hence superior to a council, especiallly in matters of faith and the governing of the Church. It was necessary to reconcile this position with the fact that his own position as pope was the work of a council which had deposed three other popes one of whom was certainly legitimate. With regard to Church policies, Martin undertook energetic action for civil and administrative moral healing. He reacquired all the Church territories. With great success he fought against brigandage. He was justly accused of nepotism, but he was also a munificent patron of the arts and culture. In 1423 he called the fifth Holy Year. The adventure of Joan of Arc took place during his pontificate and Martin would have wanted to save her from the stake. He did not succeed because he died first. He initiated the office of apostolic secretary which today is called the secretary of state. This office has the job of helping the pope govern the universal Church, a connecting llnk between the pope and the various ministries of the Roman Curia. He was the one to order the clergy to wear cassoks. He was buried in St. John Lateran.

207. EUGENE IV (1431-1447)

He was born Gabriele Condulmer in Venice. Thanks to being a relative of Gregory XII his career rose rapidly. He was elected pope at 48 years of age. Charitable, deeply religious, austere, he was also so very determined that it was said he did not know half-measures and sometimes not even his own limitations. He called a council in Basle which had been pre-announced by Martin V to discuss, among other things, the proposal to reunite the Greek and Latin Churches made by the Eastern Emperor John VII. The proposal interested John because he was looking for Christian allies to fight the Turks who had invaded his lands. One of the first conclusions reached by the council was a document affirming the superiority of a council to a Roman pontiff. Then there was John VII's proposal which encountered stiff resistance. On the other hand the subjects discussed were of too great a theological and disciplinary importance to imagine they could be easily resolved without much discussion: the *Filioque*, the supremacy of Rome over the other churches, the epiclesis and purgatory. But Eugene, who was authoritarian and in a hurry, and possibly because he was unhappy with the anti-papal turn the council had taken, dissolved the synod and gradually moved it closer and closer to Rome - first to Bologna, then Ferrara and finally Florence. There, in the presence of John VII, the reunion was solemnly sanctioned although it was to have a short life. Eugene's decision to change the venue of the synod irritated many of the Fathers participating who had already expressed their opinions favoring the superiority of councils over popes. Thus they determined to remain in Basle, taking on an even more anti- Roman stance. To affirm this idea they went into a kind of conclave where they deposed Eugene and elected a new pope, Amadeus VIII, duke of Savoy, called The Peaceful, who was a layman and took the name of Felix V (1440). He was the last anti-pope in history. The Council of Florence took the exactly opposite position to the one in Basle: that the pope is superior to a council. Eugene was a good lover and patron of the arts. He had the Pantheon and the Colosseum restored and had the central door of the Vatican basilica made in bronze.

208. NICHOLAS V (1447-1455)

He was born Tommaso Parentucelli November 15, 1397 at Sarzana in Liguria. The last anti-pope in history, Felix V, made submission to him (1449). Nicholas made him a cardinal and named him papal legate to Savoy. In 1450 he called a Holy Year during which there was an outbreak of cholera so that all the pilgrims left Rome. Thanks to his diplomatic gifts he obtained good results politically: a positive solution to the Basle schism with the resignation of the anti-pope Felix is in large part the work of the pope. He drafted a treaty with Frederick III of Austria in which the rights and privileges of the Church are regulated along with those of the Empire. Frederick was crowned emperor again in St. Peter's Basilica. He was less diplomatic with regard to the plot of a certain Stefano Porcari who wanted to restore the Roman Republic. Porcari and his conspirators were hanged at Castel Sant'Angelo. During his pontificate (1453) the Eastern Roman Empire came to an end when Mohammed II captured Constantinople and Constantine XII, the last emperor, was killed. Nicholas was a man with wide knowledge and attentive to the new cultural exigencies of the period. He too was infected with the humanistic fervor that was raging. He called a great crowd of intellectuals and artists to Rome and began a rich program of restoration of ancient monuments and modern constructions, among them St. Peter's Basilica. For that project Bramante made a grandiose design once it was decided to abandon the idea of restoring the crumbling old edifice of Constantine's. He gathered together in the Vatican all the church offices and brought the two Lateran libraries there as well which was the start of the famous Vatican Library. He took particular care of the defensive works of Church territories, renewing and fortifying many sites and cities of the Papal State. As he died he was assisted by only two Carthusian monks since he did not trust his relatives any more.

209. CALLISTUS III (1455-1458)

He was born Alfonso Borgia near Valencia, Spain on December 31, 1378. He was a famous jurist and became a councillor to King Alfonso V of Aragon. His friend St. Vincent Ferrer had predicted his election to the papacy long before. He was obsessed with the idea of recapturing Constantinople and the Holy Land and defeating the Turks who were a threat not only to the religion but also to the commerce and economy of the Christian peoples. He tried to convince the Christian princes, urging them to unite against the common enemy. Not many gave him heed, so he himself armed a fleet that cruised up and down the Mediterranean and the Aegean on the look-out for Turkish ships. He had considerable success. He also organized a land army that beat the Turks at Belgrade (1456). In memory of the victory Callistus established the holiday of the Transfiguration and ordered the recitation of the Angelus every day at noon to the sound of church bells. He gladly accepted and gave support to anyone who would adhere to his battle plans against the Turks - in particular the Albanian hero George Castriota Skanderberg who opposed the Ottomans in the Balkans. He declared the innocence of Joan of Arc who had been burned at the stake as a witch and a heretic. Callistus practised nepotism and made his family's fortune through concessions and protection. He made his nephew Rodrigo a cardinal, the infamous Alexander VI "Borgia", a symbol of dissolution, intrigue and unscrupulousness, the father of Cesare and Lucretia. Callistus died on the Transfiguration holiday which he himself had established.

210. PIUS II (1458-1464)

He was born Enea Silvio Piccolomini in Corsignano, Tuscany on October 18, 1405. Before entering the Church he had the most varied kind of experiences, some of them questionable and not very edifying. He was a great and convinced humanist who attended the Council of Basle and sided with the schismatics. The anti-pope Felix V (Amadeus VIII of Savoy) had him for a councillor and later he entered the service of Frederick III of Germany. The latter sent Pius as his ambassador to Rome. There, with unerring instinct and remarkable opportunism he publicly confessed his errors and entered on an ecclesiastical career. His rise was rapid and at 53 he was already pope. His election was greeted with enthusiasm by all humanists who saw in him the confirmation of all the cultural and artistic ideals of their movement. But he disappointed all their expectations: his only interest was to leave his indelible mark on history, not through memorable works or actions, but simply through his personality. Nevertheless he was not lacking in some merit: he canonized St. Catherine of Siena; he instituted the corps of abridgers whose job was to edit, collect and correct the petitions of the people to the pope and all Church documents; he planned serious Church reforms but found the cardinals stubbornly opposed. Following a typical Renaissance idea - the construction of a perfect city according to the classical canons of Vitruvius - he transformed his birth place, Corsignano, into that small town which today is called Pienza after his papal name. He was a quite good writer and wrote several historical works. But his biggest enterprize was the organization of a holy war against the Turks. For this purpose he tried to make an alliance with Louis XI of France, Philip of Burgundy, the king of Hungary, and Venice. Things dragged on listlessly so that after five years he himself decided to lead an army that was ready to leave. But death reached him at Ancona as he was about to set sail for the Holy Land.

211. PAUL II (1464-1471)

He was born Pietro Barbo in Venice Feb. 23, 1417 and was the nephew of Eugene IV who made him a cardinal at only 23 years of age. He was 48 when elected pope. The first problem he had to face was the thorny one of the Turks who had advanced into Christian territory. In vain he tried to sew together an alliance. But he did have success with the Albanian hero George Castriota Skanderberg who fought to liberate his homeland with the valid help of Paul II. He took up again the construction of St. Peter's Basilica entrusting the work to Giuliano da Sangallo. He imposed papal power on Rome in an authoritarian manner replacing "Consuls" with "Curators", the latter being strictly dependent on the Church unlike the former. To make up for the discontent he created, he presented the Roman populace with the "Golden Rose" as a sign of favored status and saw to it that each month a sufficient sum of money was given to the poor. He ruled that a Holy Year was to be held every 25 years. Paul, who mainly worked at night, died suddenly at a relatively young age.

212. SIXTUS IV (1471-1484)

Francesco della Rovere was born at Celle near Savona on July 21, 1414. He became general of the Franciscan order a great preacher and famous theologian. He also greatly practised nepotism to the point of scandal: to aid and cover up the great turmoil provoked by his nephews he did not hesitate to make enemies of Florence, Naples, Ferrara and Venice. He got involved, for example, in the Pazzi conspiracy against the Medicis in Florence. The plot, which aimed at the deaths of Lorenzo and Giuliano dei Medici, was ordered by his nephew Cardinal Riario. The plot failed. One of the victims of the Medici's vengeance was Bishop Salviati of Pisa who had been active in the conspiracy. He was killed and his body hung from a window. Sixtus, in cahoots with the king of Naples, acted against Florence in his nephew's defence and to demand satisfaction for the profanation of a priest of the Church. The affair ended in a peace treaty in memory of which the pope had the Church of Santa Maria della Pace built in Rome. In 1475 he held a Holy Year. He was the first pope to give official approval to the San Giuseppe holiday on March 19.

213. INNOCENT VIII (1484-1492)

He was born Giovanni Battista Cybo in Genoa in 1432. His ecclesiastical career started late after a dissipated and pleasure-seeking life. His election was unquestionably the result of compromises and intrigues. After election his first concern was to recognize two illegitimate children, Teodorina and Franceschetto, covering them with benefits and privileges. Behavior that would be considered a scandal today was fairly well tolerated by all of society in those times. The Christian recapture of Granada, the last Arab fortress in Europe, put the pope into a euphoric state so that he bestowed the title of "Catholic" on Spain's King Ferdinand. Innocent received as a gift the lance which had pierced the ribs of Christ, conserved today in St. Peter's Basilica. He depleted the entire treasury of the Church to satisfy the greed of the Curia which controlled him completely so that he was unable to deny them anything. His name is infamously tied to the document that he signed at the request of the German inquisitors authorizing a witch hunt. He condemned Pico della Mirandola as a heretic and prohibited him from discussing his 900 theses. This philosopher had advanced the hypothesis of a rigid ecclesiastical reform and had theorized that it was impossible to base Christian faith on classical philosophy. Innocent however was a Renaissance man and therefore open to scientific ideas: he was the first man known to have undergone a blood transfusion in the attempt to be cured of his physical ailments. He had always been ailing. He died shortly after the blood transfusion on the eve of the discovery of America. To his credit, he used his influence with King Ferdinand of Spain to induce him to help Christopher Columbus realize his venture.

214. ALEXANDER VI (1492-1503)

Rodrigo Borgia was born at Jàtiva near Valencia, Spain on January 11, 1431. He was the nephew of of Callistus III who made him a cardinal when he was only 25 years old. He is the pope who in the popular imagination is the symbol of corruption, intrigue, a total lack of scruples and morality. He has been charged, sometimes unjustly or in a highly exaggerated way, with the most horrendous and loathsome crimes. Critical historians have re-evaluated his case as well as doing justice to his much-slandered daughter Lucretia. It appears harder to rehabilitate his other child, Cesare, greedy, violent and unscrupulous for whose sake Alexander compromised himself in order to create a kingdom made to his measure. He supported Cesare in the project to conquer Italian cities and ruling councils which he intended to unite under his rule. To this end he even sought the help of his enemy Charles VIII of France. Once he no longer needed him, however, he became the enemy of Charles again and fought him with every means at his disposal. Alexander tried to put together alliances against him, even to the point of making pacts with the Turks. At first things did not go well for Alexander, but in the long run he managed to turn the situation around, transforming a heavy defeat into a resounding victory: Charles was obliged to return over the Alps to France. In 1500 he celebrated a holy year. He had a sumptuous apartment built for himself in the Vatican decorated by Pinturicchio. America was discovered during his papacy. As soon as the news reached him, Alexander sent three bulls to Ferdinand and Isabella authorizing them to reign over the newly discovered islands and the lands still to be discovered. But John II of Portugal also had claims granted him by Eugene IV. The dispute was resolved by Alexander in Solomon-like fashion and very simply: as is well known he drew a line on the map dividing the world into two parts, one of which he assigned to Spain and the other to Portugal. That is the origin of the present situation in Latin America. An old story says that the two sovereigns in recompense sent the pope the first gold obtained in America which he used to decorate the ceiling of the basilica of Santa Maria Maggiore. Alexander was hated by the Roman populace and patricians for a number of justifiable reasons: nepotism, corruption, luxury, arrogance, brazen favoritism of the Spanish to the detriment of the local people. The Dominican monk Gerolamo Savanarola preached against him, his children and the Curia. Alexander tried to win him over without success. So he excommunicated him and had him burned alive in Florence in 1498. Everyone was waiting for the pope to die, each for his own reasons. His death came abruptly on August 18, 1503. Popular imagination would have one believe he died when poison he intended for someone else was mistakenly administered to him.

215. PIUS III (1503)

He was born Francesco Todeschini-Piccolomini in Siena in 1439. He was the nephew of Pius II and by papal decree was allowed to join Pius II's family name to his own. His life was marked by honesty and piety. He was among the adversaries of Alexander VI to whom he refused to sell his vote. He was already old and suffering from gout when the conclave nominated him to the papacy. Conscious of his limitations he refused several times, but the College of Cardinals insisted. His was a very short papacy lasting only 26 days in which he did not have the chance to do anything at all despite the best of intentions.

216. JULIUS II (1503-1513)

He was born Giuliano Della Rovere near Savona on December 5, 1443. He was a nephew of Sixtus IV and an implacable enemy of Alexander VI whose election he had fought against twelve years earlier. This was certainly not from jealousy. Rather his conception of life and of the Church was absolutely antithetical to his predecessor's. During all the time Alexander was pope, Cardinal Giuliano Della Rovere refused to set foot in Rome and remained in Ostia in the castle he had had built there. His aversion to Borgia was so intense that when he became pope he could not bring himself to live in the same apartment, magnificently decorated by Pinturicchio, where Alexander had resided. His first objective as pope was to restore the pontifical finances squandered during the Borgia decade. In politics he switched alliances from France to Spain, only concerned with watching out for the interests of the Church and making sure that his allies did not become too powerful to his own detriment. An astute strategist and ambitious politician, he dreamed of an Italy united under the sovereignity of the Roman pontiff which could claim a guiding role and primacy over all the other European states. Naturally he encountered opposition and hostility, above all from Louis XII of France. Julius II was a great patron of the arts even if it is said he paid the artists badly. As is well known, Michelangelo had to put up with this with whom he had turbulent relations, sometimes capricious and insolent, but also full of esteem and admiration. Under his auspices the artist completed the decorations for the ceiling of the Sistine Chapel while Bramante was commissioned to continue with the construction of St. Peter's Basilica. He commissioned Raphael to paint the Loggias and the Stanze which he had built above the famous Borgia aparment and where he lived. In 1506 he made The Swiss Guards an official corp - something which Sixtus IV had already decided to do - with the job of protecting the pope's person and his territories. Julius II is buried in St. Peter's Basilica. His funeral monument, which he personally commissioned from Michelangelo, was to be a grandiose work projected for a central place in the Vatican basilica. It was never finished due to lack of funds and the only remnant of it is the statue of Moses in the church of San Pietro in Vincoli.

217. LEO X (1513-1521)

He was born Giovanni dei Medici in Florence on December 11, 1475. At the age of 13 he was already a cardinal and was elected pope at 38. His pontificate is remembered as a splendid period culturally and artistically with a court that hosted the best artists and most eminent minds of the time: Raphael, Bramante, Michelangelo, Bembo, Pico della Mirandola. There they found unlimited possibilities for creative expression as well as luxury and entertainment. Leo himself made the remark: "Let us enjoy the papacy, for God has conferred it upon us". And the entire pontifical court shared his feelings. But his name is even more closely connected to Martin Luther's Protestant reform. Spurred by Leo's sale of indulgences to raise funds to finance the construction of St. Peter's, the Augustinian monk published his famous 95 theses and began spreading them by means of assiduous preaching. This was the last straw that led to rebellion and reform. The roots were more extensive and went further back: the scandalous vice in which primarily men of the Church lived with utter indifference, treading even the most basic principles of a Christian life under foot. The reform spread rapidly, heeded by princes and peoples. Luther was called to Rome to defend himself, but he disobeyed and the pope excommunicated him. Leo X introduced the Index - the list of books that Catholics were prohibited from reading. Like almost all the popes of this period, he put the papacy at the disposition of his family interests and favored the family's return to Florence by granting his nephew Lorenzo the duchy of Urbino. He deposed four cardinals involved in a conspiracy against him. In their place he created 31 new cardinals to counterbalance the thirteen who made up the Sacred College with which he was discontented. He never took sides completely with either Francis I of France or Charles V of Spain, but allied himself with one or the other from time to time as it served his interests. He died suddenly, possibly from poisoning.

218. HADRIAN VI (1522-1523)

He was born Adrian Florensz in Utrecht in Holland on March 2, 1459. He did not change his name upon being elected. He had been rector of the University of Louvain from which post the Emperor Maximilian took him to tutor his grandson, the little Charles V. He was also the teacher of Erasmus of Rotterdam and grand inquisitor and then governor of Spain. It was this last office that he was performing when he was elevated to the papacy "because of his immaculate life". He responded with enthusiasm and commitment for the good of the Church. But in Rome, besides plague, he found a hostile reception. An austere character, he was demanding of himself and others. He tried to raise the moral level of the Curia without success. He put into effect a policy of economizing and applied it to everything, not only reducing wastefullness, but also cutting necessary expenditures such as funds for the fight against the Protestant Reformation. He did not accept the biting ironic spirit of the Roman populace and he prohibited many of their customs, even innocent ones, even to the point of condemning to death Pasquino who was the spirit incarnate of the people's most authentic self expression. Fortunately the condemnation was never carried out. In this way he made many enemies among both the powerful and the people. Thus the doctor who treated him in his final illness - possibly with intentional neglect - was hailed as the saviour of the country. But many in the Church considered him a saint. He called for the Diet of Nuremberg where his spokesman admitted the culpability of the Church, hoping in this way to win the land back to Catholicism. He tried to reconcile France and Spain to induce them to fight the Turks who were again representing a threat. And he wrote constantly to Frederick of Saxony, Luther's protector, urging him to renounce the latter's teachings.

219. CLEMENT VII (1523-1534)

He was born Giulio dei Medici in Florence on May 26, 1479. He was a cousin of Leo X and nephew of Lorenzo the Magnificent. Clement was pope at a dramatic time in the history of the Church: the Lutheran revolt had reached its climax putting the papacy and Catholicism to a very hard test. Clement did not prove up to the job, not understanding the gravity of the situation. His actions were weak and he only moved to defend his family's private interests. In the contest between Charles V and Francis I for supremacy in Europe, Clement took the side of Francis who had promised to support the Medicis' return to power in Florence. In so doing Clement broke a previous agreement between Charles V and Hadrian VI. In the war that followed the French king got the worst of it and was beaten in the battle of Pavia. Charles V punished the pope's treachery in an exemplary manner: he set the Landsknechte, German mercenaries, upon Rome (1527) who sacked it ferociously for six months. Peace was made in Barcelona. Charles V promised to help the Medicis to return to Florence and Clement in exchange recognized him as emperor. At first Charles condemned Lutheranism and prohibited its practise. But later, struck by the vociferous protests of the Lutheran princes - thus the name "protestants" - and from fear of remaining isolated, he permitted the new cult to be active. But for the majority of the princes, adherence to Lutheranism was only a pretext for taking possession of Church and monastery property. It is obvious that Charles was inspired by political reasons and not religious convictions. Henry VIII of England also provoked the split with Rome. His reason was the pope's refusal to grant him a divorce from Catherine of Aragon so that he could marry Anne Boleyn. The English king went much farther than the other European sovereigns: he named himself spiritual head of the English Church and threatened with death all of his subjects who rejected his reform.

220. PAUL III (1534-1549)

He was born Alessandro Farnese in Rome on February 29, 1468. His life was worldly and fun-filled. He had three children from as many women. At 26 Alexander VI made him a cardinal, but he received no religious orders - the office of cardinal being honorific, it can also be given to laymen. He had no interest whatsoever in an ecclesiastical career. But at the age of 46 he withdrew from the world entirely, took religious orders and led an upright life. A cultivated man, clever at politics, he enjoyed the esteem of the popes and the Curia. This made his election fast and unanimous. His program can be summarized in three points: "eliminate the schism, reform the Church and fight the Turks." The enormous problems that had afflicted earlier popes only got worse during his pontificate. To Luther, Zwingli and Henry VIII, there was now added Calvin in Switzerland and other European countries. Calvin preached an even more rigid and intransigent reform. Catholicism was under attack from various sides, even by those monarchs who had remained Catholic. Everyone took advantage of the opportunity to shake off the religious, political and financial conditions that the Church had imposed in the past and which were unwillingly supported. Paul III took the Protestant Reformation very seriously and faced the problem from two sides, the doctrinal and the pastoral aspects. On the one hand he convened the Council of Trent (1542) which had already been announced. Including all of its suspensions the council lasted eighteen years. It reaffirmed the traditional Catholic faith by systematically confuting all the Protestant propositions. Paul III went farther: he arranged for the doctrinal proclamations to be accompanied by intense pastoral propagandizing for the Catholic heritage, for which purpose it created the Holy Office and a new religious order: the Company of Jesus. To oppose the heresy it also tried the road of politics, trying to make peace between Charles V and Francis I for the purpose of creating a united front against the Protestants. It tried to radically reform the Church beginning with the Curia. In a word, it began that reaction of the Catholic Church which is called the Counter-Reformation. It was accused of nepotism and with reason. But it always had at heart the good of the Church and of Rome where it commissioned many works. Outstanding are the commissions it gave to Michelangelo: the project for the Campidoglio, the grandiose Last Judgement fresco in the Sistine Chapel, the dome of St. Peter's and the Farnese Palace in Rome. Paul III was esteemed by many scientists and writers of the time.

221. JULIUS III (1550-1555)

He was born Giovanni Maria Ciocchi Del Monte in Rome on September 10, 1487. Despite the very serious situation, his first thought was to enjoy life among banqueting, hunting and court jesters. But he quickly realized that he would have to change his course. Therefore he reopened the Council of Trent which continued for several sessions and then was immediately suspended due to the conflicts and the war that broke out between Charles V and Francis I. He tried very hard to bring back peace with a policy of conciliation which, however, was unsuccessful. Meanwhile the Protestant Reformation had spread to Scotland and France too where they were called Huguenots. Julius approved the founding of a university by St. Ignatius Loyola, the Gregorian University, which was later to be extended by Pope Gregory XIII and to take his name. Like many popes of the time, he too practised nepotism. It created a scandal when he nominated cardinal the 17-year-old Innocent Del Monte, a foundling adopted by one of Julius's brothers. He confirmed and celebrated the 1550 Holy Year that Paul III had called for.

222. MARCELLUS II (1555)

Marcello Cervini came from Montepulciano di Siena where he was born on May 6, 1501. After election he kept his baptismal name and was the last pope to do so. He was pope for only 22 days during which he distinguished himself for his charity and good behavior. He made a particularly courageous gesture in ordering that of the expenses foreseen for the coronation half should go to the poor and the other half to the Church. He intended this as an example of austerity for the Curia. He was so much against nepotism that he forbade his relatives to come to Rome. He died from the strain of the pontificate possibly aggravated by a sore on his leg of which no one knew anything. Pier Luigi da Palestrina composed the famous *Messa Papa Marcello* for him.

223. PAUL IV (1555-1559)

He was born Gian Pietro Carafa near Benevento on June 28, 1476. As a bishop he founded, together with San Gaetano (Cajetan) da Thiene, the Theatine order for the care of the sick and the injured. Ascetic, energetic, inflexible to the point of being fanatic, he girded himself for the struggle for Church reform of which he had always dreamed. Harsh provisions radically changed the Curia and the life of the religious orders. He used coercive methods to reach his goals even with illustrious personages. Today one would say that he was no respecter of persons. And he was just as hard towards the Protestants. The main tool he used in his fight was the court of the Inquisition which he activated and organized. He applied it equally against Catholics or Protestants. These were years of terror: torture was used with unnatural ease to extort confessions. Mary Tudor, the daughter of Henry VIII and Catherine of Aragon, practised the same incredible ferocity on Anglicans. When she took the throne of England she tried to restore Catholicism with such terrorist methods that she became known as "bloody Mary". But her plan did not work because her sister Elizabeth I who succeeded her returned to the Anglican faith founded by her father. Paul VI was intransigent and intolerant with the Jewish community which had lived in Rome since ancient Roman times. He raised their taxes and banned them from practising any art or profession, from acquiring real estate, and prohibited Jewish doctors from treating Christian patients. He also ordered them to live in a ghetto where the gates were closed at night and it was hard to get out. Thus it is natural that the Jews hailed his death as a liberation. Paul developed Marcel II's idea of a printing establishment that later became the famous "Poliglotta Vaticana". His secretary was Mnsr. Della Casa author of the celebrated book of Italian etiquette "Il Galateo". Paul died of dropsy. The news spread rapidly and provoked an uprising among the people who occupied the Palace of the Inquisition, freed the prisoners, and set it on fire, after which they pulled down the statue of the pope that stood in the Campidoglio.

224. PIUS IV (1560-1565)

He was born Giovan Angelo dei Medici in Milan on March 31, 1499. He was in no way a relation of the Florentine Medicis, but the duke of Tuscany invited him to take over their coat-of-arms. They managed to agree on his election because he was a mild man and considered to represent no danger either for the Spanish or the French. But in the end he took the side of Spain and made no bones about it. Even while alleviating some of the harshness of Paul III's decrees, he continued to reform the Church in a rigorous and consistent manner. He even concerned himself with reopening the Council of Trent (1562) and bringing it to a conclusion (1563). All the dogmas of the Catholic faith were reaffirmed and consequently condemned the Protestant Reformation in all of its ramifications. In particular it forcefully proclaimed the supreme authority of the Roman pontiff. It also launched a reform in ecclesiastical discipline, condemned simony and the sale of indulgences. In short, a great effort was made to correct the errors that had brought about the Protestant schism. Furthermore it decided to adopt a system for opposing Turkish raiders. Because of the regime Pius imposed on the Curia, his Spanish sympathies and the heaviness of his fiscal policies, a conspiracy was hatched against him, but he managed to escape with his life. His nephews were Carlo and Federico Borromeo both of whom he made cardinals and archbishops in Milan. He also concerned himself with the urbanistic aspects of Rome and Papal State. Among his enterprizes stand out the construction of the church of Santa Maria degli Angeli in Rome which Michelangelo extracted from the Baths of Diocletian. By his express desire, Pius was buried there.

225. PIUS V, St. (1566-1572)

He was born Antonio Michele Ghisleri near Alessandria on January 17, 1504. He was a Dominican friar and even as pope he did not change his austere style of life. The objective he set himself was to give full implementation to the decisions of the Council of Trent, devoting himself with particular intensity to the reform of Church customs. These had been the cause of the Protestant Reformation and that was the point at which one had to begin. He therefore decreed rigid norms of morality and discipline for priests, gave strong impetus to seminaries, organizing the studies in a way to guarantee that the new priests would be not only endowed with good morals but a good education. For this purpose he published the Roman Catechism, an easy-to-consult manual intended primarily for parish priests, a kind of *summa* of the orthodox faith. He ordered the official adoption of the Roman missal. To make reform action more incisive, he made wide use of the court of the Inquisition in those cases where it encountered excessive and culpable opposition. He revised the Index of prohibited books, giving it a definitive form. He excommunicate Elizabeth I of England who had restored the Anglican faith. During his papacy a great historical event for the Church and the entire West took place: the battle of Lepanto in 1571 when the Christian fleet defeated the Turkish one thus initiating the definitive decline of Islamic power. In memory of that victory, Pius V established the holiday of Santa Maria della Vittoria or del Rosario. His remains are venerated in the Sistine Chapel of the church of Santa Maria Maggiore.

226. GREGORY XIII (1572-1585)

He was born Ugo Boncompagni in Bologna on January 1, 1502. Before becoming pope he had a son, Giacomo. He was so generally esteemed that the conclave to elect him took only one day. During his pontificate the various Roman factions again took on vigor and arrogance led by the usual patrician families who would not put up with, among other things, the austerity Gregory had imposed on Roman life. The pope had proposed to carry on with the projects for the reform of the institutions and customs in the spirit of the Council of Trent. But Gregory did not have the energy to impose them. On the contrary, he practised nepotism despite his proposals of austerity. He made various nephews into cardinals and his son Giacomo the governor of the Castel Sant'Angelo. In politics his actions were rather ineffective and he made some errors of judgement. For example, he received with gratification the news of the St. Bartholomew massacre (1570) of the Huguenots, wrongly imagining that this would lead to new religious peace in France. He fostered and aided financially Philip II of Spain's wars against England, imagining that in this way Catholicism could be restored in that country. He even went so far as to approve a plot for the assassination of Queen Elizabeth I. His merits must be sought for elsewhere, in the interest he took in culture and science. He fostered the studies of the clergy by establishing seminaries, colleges and schools - the Collegio Romano and the Gregorian University. He had a great passion for astronomy and had the Tower of the Winds built within the Vatican walls which was the nucleus of that famous observatory which today is located at Castel Gandolfo. The most important scientists of the epoch met within that tower to study and expound the results of their research. These gave rise to the revised calendar which is the pope's greatest glory. The old Julian calendar was abandoned and the new Gregorian one adopted (1582) which today is in use all over the world. He built on the Quirinal Hill the palace of the same name as a summer residence for the pope.

227. SIXTUS V (1585-1590)

He was born Felice Peretti in Grottamare (Ancona) on December 13, 1521. He was a Franciscan friar and general of the order. Legend states that he entered the conclave decrepit and bent over, but on being elected he straightened up proudly and looked in perfect physical health. In politics, despite mutual dislike, he was the ally of Philip II of Spain with whom he undertook several projects all of which failed: they did not manage to stop the Calvinist Henry of Navara from taking the throne of France and had to watch the invincible armada (1588) sink along with the dream of a restoration of Catholicism in England. Against nepotism, austere, severe and endowed with a will of iron, he continued inflexibly imposing the reforms already begun on religious orders, nobles and Christian communities without any exceptions. The methods used were terrible and pitiless: two scaffolds were always ready in front of Castel Sant'Angelo, and not only as a warning. The condemned were many and the victims came from every social class without distinction: criminals, brigands and nobles. The results were brilliant: brigandage was wiped out and Rome and the Papal State became more peaceful and safe than they had ever been. Despite all of this Sixtus was not much loved, probably because he impinged upon too many private interests. In fact, when he died, riots broke out and his statue in the Campidoglio risked being pulled down. He was deeply concerned with urbanistic questions and had a regulating plan drawn up with the four largest basilicas pin-pointed as sites for development. Many were the public works undertaken: four obelisks in four squares were righted. Well known is the story of the Genoese sailor whose call to danger saved the obelisk in St. Peter's Square from a disastrous fall. He opened straight new streets, finished the dome of St. Peter's in record time, finished work on the Quirinal Palace and the Felice aqueduct; he built the new Vatican Apostolic Palace and another at St. John Lateran's beside which he had the famous Holy Steps set up; he consecrated the Trinità dei Monti Church. He set the number of cardinals at 70. He died in the very new Quirinal Palace and was buried in Santa Maria Maggiore.

228. URBAN VII (1590)

He was born Giovanni Battista Castagna in Rome on August 4, 1521. His was a good and charitable nature and he began his pontificate with several memorable actions: the compilation of a list of poor families to be helped; ordered the Holy See to cover part of the debts contracted by individuals of the populace at the pawn institution Monte di Pietà; offered a large sum of his own money to establish a fund for poor girls without dowries. He did not have time to fulfil any of these projects, but the intention was enough to make the people love and mourn for him. He died suddenly of malaria.

229. GREGORY XIV (1590-1591)

His name was NiccolÚ Sfondrati and he was born at Somma in Lombardy on February 11, 1535. He was urged to dedicate himself to the Church by St. Charles Borromeo and was a friend of St. Philip Neri and St. Louis Gonzaga. A profoundly pious and humble man, he was a mystic by nature and much more given to pastoral work than to government and politics. In poor health all his life, he gave over the governing of the city to a nephew, young, greedy and inexperienced, whom he made his secretary of state. He sided with Philip II of Spain and against Henry IV of France whom he excommunicated for having supported and protected the French Protestants. Gregory tried unsuccessfully to form an alliance against Henry. He loved the people whom he protected and fed, especially in a time of famine and pestilence. He died after only a ten-months reign.

230. INNOCENT IX (1591-1591)

Gian Antonio Facchinetti was born in Bologna on July 20, 1519. He was a good and meek man, but also a very capable diplomat. Pius V sent him as papal nuncio to Venice to equip the fleet of the Holy League that was to defeat the Turks at Lepanto in 1571. When he was elected he was already old and ill. He spent the two months of his pontificate in bed and was nicknamed *pontifex clinicus*. For the rest it was a very gloomy time with an outbreak of plague. He barely had the time to begin putting the ruined Vatican finances in order and to make some decrees regarding public order. Before dying he provided for two nephews, one of whom he made a cardinal and the other supreme commander of the fleet.

231. CLEMENT VIII (1592-1605)

He was born Ippolito Aldobrandini at Fano to an important Florentine family on February 24, 1536. He was unanimously elected pope against his will. Exquisite, cultivated, with clean habits, he yet practised nepotism to an extreme degree. That is the only thing that could be said against him aside from a tendency to luxury. For the rest he concerned himself with the well-being of the people and the reform of the Church in obedience to the rulings of the Council of Trent. He managed to make peace between Spain and France, thus creating the basis for a period of stability in Europe. He removed the excommunication from Henry IV after he publicly abjured Protestanism which he had previously accepted and favored. As a consequence of this peace with France, the Protestants' freedom of worship was recognized and Catholicism restored. In 1600, while the Holy Year was celebrated with great pomp, Clement condemned the philosopher Giordano Bruno, a Dominican monk, to burn at the stake for having opposed some Church doctrines. Clement also was a patron of the arts and artists. At Frascati, outside Rome, he had a sumptuous villa built as a summer residence. He died suddenly, possibly from apoplexy while attending a session of the court of the Inquisition.

232. LEO XI (1605)

He was born Alessandro dei Medici in Florence on June 2, 1535. In the conclave, he won out over the famous Cardinal Baronio, who was the favored candidate. As a true ascetic, he was good and generous with others while being very hard on himself. He was an enemy of nepotism. His very brief papacy lasted hardly 27 days during which time he concerned himself with coming to the aid of the imperial army fighting the Turks in Hungary. He died a few days after falling from a horse while riding to the Lateran to take possession of it and to be crowned.

233. PAUL V (1605-1621)

Camillo Borghese was born either in Rome or Siena on September 17, 1552. A good jurist and esteemed diplomat, he was elected during a tormented and tempestuous conclave. He practised the most extreme kind of nepotism and maintained a pontifical court as luxurious and generous as had been the custom in his family. Despite all that he governed justly and firmly. When it was necessary to defend the interests of the Church he fought with courage and determination.

Typical is the story of his quarrel with Venice where on two occasions the rights of the Church had been trampled on. In the first case two clerics had been tried and condemned by a civilian court rather than being turned over to the papal nuncio; in the second, the civil authorities had prohibited the building of churches without their permission and donations and inheritances in favor of the Church had been prohibited. Paul laid an interdict on the city and excommunicated doge and senate. Venice responded by unleashing polemics that agitated all Europe for two years. There was a famous debate between Roberto Bellarmino who took the side of the pope, and Paolo Sarpi who defended Venice. In the end the dispute was settled thanks to the intervention of Henry of Navarra with neither winners nor losers, but seriously prejudicial to papal authority which was judged to be too absolutist even by some Catholics. Today what appears to be a serious blemish on Paul V was his confirmation of the Inquisition's condemnation of Copernicus's theories considered stupid, inconclusive and contrary to the Scriptures. Paul V was another pope who took great care of the urbanistic aspect of Rome. He rendered great service to the city by restoring Trajan's aqueduct that brought water from Lake Bracciano and the Aurelian Way to the Trastevere quarter of the city. He was a great patron of the arts. His favorite artists were Guido Reni and Carlo Maderno whom he commissioned to design the imposing facade of St. Peter's Basilica. Paul V was buried in the church of Santa Maria Maggiore.

234. GREGORY XV (1621-1623)

He was born Alessandro Ludovisi in Bologna on January 9, 1554. The conclave that elected him was short and being outside all partisan politics Ludovisi was unopposed. Gregory was not physically strong and called on his energetic nephew Ludovico, whom he had made cardinal, to help him govern. He concerned himself with giving a permanent form to the laws of conclaves and this remained in force until the time of Pope Paul VI. The cardinals were particularly prohibited from lending themselves to the political power games of the European states and secrecy was recommended. Gregory founded the Congregation for the Propaganda of the Faith for the purpose of fostering and coordinating the missions scattered throughout the world. To give it a worthy headquarters he had a palace constructed near Piazza di Spagna designed by Bernini and Borromini. He canonized St. Philip Neri, St. Teresa and St. Francis Saverio. He was not immune from the vice of nepotism. He was buried in the Roman church of Sant'Ignazio which his nephew, Cardinal Ludovisi, had had built for the Jesuits.

235. URBAN VIII (1623-1644)

Maffeo Barberini was born in Florence in 1568. He was educated by the Jesuits and his election took him so much by surprize that he himself asked for a new vote. He was unanimously confirmed. He was a brilliant and cultivated man. Although practising extreme nepotism, he did not allow his relatives to interfere in the affairs of the Church. Otherwise he favored and protected them in every possible way. He condemned the Jansenist theories and it was during his reign that Gallileo, who supported the Copernican heliocentric theory, was condemned. The great astronomer was forced to disavow his ideas to save his life. The pope protected him by commuting the sentence inflicted by the Inquisition from life in prison to exile in Arcetri. Urban's construction and urbanistic work was vast and important. He had the Pantheon restored, but had the bronze removed from the beams of the portico which Bernini than used to make the monumental spiral columns for his famous baldachin in St. Peter's. He had the great Barberini palace built which today houses an important art collection. He extended and fortified the encircling walls of Rome. The papal villa at Castel Gandolfo, with an ample park and ancient trees which ever since has been the summer residence of the popes, was commissioned by him. But despite his merits the populace did not mourn his passing, remembering the high taxation imposed to finance his public and private works. Urban ordained no less than 78 cardinals including the famous Mazarin who was the French prime minister.

236. INNOCENT X (1644-1655)

He was born Giovanni Battista Pamphili in Rome on May 7, 1574. As soon as he was elected he put the Barberinis on trial for abuses committed under Urban VIII, but he abandoned it quickly for fear of reprisals from the French who were great friends of theirs. He supported the Venetians in their war against the Turks and saw the Thirty Years War end with the victory of the Protestant states. Under the urging of 80 French cardinals, he again condemned the Jansenist doctrines on grace and predestination. A woman it was who dominated the Roman scene in those days: Olimpia Maidalchini, the pope's sister-in-law. Ambitious, greedy and an intriguer she filled up all the space in Roman political and social life becoming the most important figure in the Curia. From that vantage point she maneuvered people and events at will, provoking many incidents and causing the pope much displeasure who nevertheless protected her. Innocent celebrated the Holy Year of 1650 with great pomp. Intelligent, open and sensitive, he took to heart the trials of the most unfortunate and the weakest. He built new prisons on humane principles that were very uncommon for those days. He wrote to the Russian Czar Alexei proclaiming the cause of the serfs and demanding their enfranchisement. Bernin, Borromini and other noted artists created noble and highly popular works for him, including the baroque setting of Piazza Navona and redoing the interior of the basilica of St. John Lateran and Villa Pamphili on the Janiculum Hill. It is said that when he died his body was left unattended for three days and no one concerned themselves with the funeral except a few workers who composed the corpse and held vigil over it. Only afterwards did his relatives provide for the funeral. The much-loved Olimpia did not lift a finger.

237. ALEXANDER VII (1655-1667)

Fabio Chigi was born in Siena on Feb. 13, 1599. His pontificate was tormented by controversies with Louis XIV of France and Cardinal Mazarin who had attempted to establish an independent national Church in France. On various occasions Alexander was forced to submit to humiliations from the French. He opposed and condemned the Jansenist ideas that had made remarkable headway in France. He fostered the interests of his relatives allowing them to increase the family wealth - already great - beyond all reasonable bounds. He welcomed the new Catholic convert, Queen Christina of Sweden, to Rome and invited her to stay. She had recently abdicated her throne to devote herself entirely to religion. She always enjoyed his favor, even on occasions when she created problems for him. He was a connoisseur of art and a generous patron to artists with whom he liked to meet to discuss ideas and solutions. It was probably he who gave Bernini the idea for the monumental colonnade that encloses St. Peter's Square. And he actively collaborated in thinking up the festive "Gloria" that adorns the apse of St. Peter's Basilica. He founded the university library (the "Alessandrina") which is still in service today.

238. CLEMENT IX (1667-1669)

He was born Giulio Rospigliosi in Pistoia on January 27, 1600. He was just as cultivated as he was generous with the poor. Each day he invited ten beggars to his table and served them himself. He reduced the fiscal burden, lowering some taxes and eliminating others. With all that, he still managed to put public finances in order. He established a new relationship with the faithful, confessing penitents personally and receiving everyone without distinction. He played an active role as mediator between France and Spain in the conflict that ended with the treaty of Aix-la-Chapelle (1668). He too practised nepotism to a degree giving his relatives important offices, but demanded that they live honest disciplined lives and content themselves with no more than reasonable compensation.

239. CLEMENT X (1670-1676)

Emilio Altieri was born in Rome on July 12, 1590. He was elected pope unexpectedly at the age of eighty. He entrusted practically everything to his nephew Cardinal Paluzzi who, acting in the pope's stead, practised the most shameless kind of nepotism and created discontent among the Curia and the people with his arrogant ways. Despite the strenuous defence of the Venetians and Clement's aid, Crete fell to the Turks. Meanwhile, Poland too was invaded. Clement supported John Sobieski in every way who moved against the Ottomans and in 1673 defeated them for the first time. He celebrated the Holy Year in 1675 with great festivity attracting enormous numbers of pilgrims to Rome.

240. INNOCENT XI, Bl. (1676-1689)

Benedetto Odescalchi was born at Como on May 19, 1611. He was elected despite having refused the nomination more than once. As pope he continued to lead the same upright life he had before his election and demanded the same from others. He was distinctly against nepotism. He took particular care in his choice of priests, wanting them honest and educated. He would remark: "Better to have fewer priests, but good ones". He destined all the massive financial resources collected from the Catholic world to help John Sobieski in a new war against the Turks. Having overrun the Balkans, they had now arrived at the gates of Vienna where the Austrian Emperor Leopold I had locked himself in. The Turks were defeated and Vienna liberated. From that moment the Turks began to lose ground in the Balkans and in Europe generally. To commemorate the Christian victory the holiday of the Holy Name of Mary was established. Innocent, like other popes before him, had to fight hard battles with Louis XIV of France. He had founded the so-called Gallican Church, independent and autonomous, with the conniving of 34 French cardinals who held an assembly and approved the four following propositions: 1) the power of the pope is limited; 2) Councils are superior to popes; 3) kings are independent of popes; 4) the king of France has a royal right to the property of the Church. Naturally all four propositions were condemned by Innocent who refused to recognize the cardinals Louis had named. Furthermore, he was much pained by the ferocious persecutions levelled at the French Protestants who had been allowed freedom of worship by Henry of Navarre. His condemnation was firm. He again condemned a new heresy: "quietism" - do nothing but wait for God to act - which at first he had favored. In governing Rome, Innocent was just and severe while combating the "laxity" of the Jesuits and other religious orders whom he urged to return to the strict observance of their rules. Pius XII proclaimed his beatification.

241. ALEXANDER VIII (1689-1691)

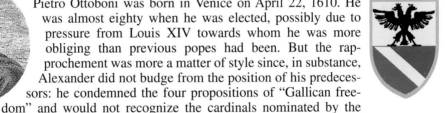

Pietro Ottoboni was born in Venice on April 22, 1610. He was almost eighty when he was elected, possibly due to pressure from Louis XIV towards whom he was more obliging than previous popes had been. But the rapprochement was more a matter of style since, in substance, Alexander did not budge from the position of his predecessors: he condemned the four propositions of "Gallican freedom" and would not recognize the cardinals nominated by the French king. He held as generous and entertaining a court as a Renaissance prince and governed the Papal State mildly, reducing taxes and allowing farmers to sell their grain freely. If exaggerated nepotism led him to commit some errors - raising unworthy relatives to high ecclesiastical and civil positions - he was, on the other hand, generous with the Church making it a gift of the library of the late Christina of Sweden which he had bought at his own expense. Under his reign banditry grew again, possibly taking advantage of his relative laxity.

242. INNOCENT XII (1691-1700)

He was born Antonio Pignatelli of a princely family at Spinazzola on March 13, 1615. Determinedly against nepotism, he made the cardinals sign a document committing themselves to fighting this ancient plague of the Church and which each new pope would be obliged to sign. This provision won him the dislike of those families which had been enriched through one of their own having been a pope, as well as the hostility of those families who hoped to put a relative on the papal throne in the future. He fought against luxurious living and concerned himself with discipline and the spiritual practices of the clergy. He obliged the latter always to wear cassocks and to do their spiritual exercises. He condemned quietism which maintained that one should abandon oneself to the actions of God and do nothing else, and that once the soul had achieved contemplation it need do no other virtuous deeds. Innocent managed to end the dispute with Louis XIV by recognizing the cardinals he had named in exchange for Louis' abjuring the four propositions of "Gallican freedom" (see Pope Innocent XI, no. 240). He fostered greatly the missions to many parts of the world and spent large amounts of money on them. He also earmarked great sums for activities and war against the old enemy Islam. For himself he reserved such a slender daily allowance that it bordered upon poverty. In this way he managed to leave his successor a real treasure - one million scudi, incredible in those days - which he kept closely guarded in the Castel Sant'Angelo. He called the Holy Year of 1700 but did not see its end because he died within the year.

243. CLEMENT XI (1700-1721)

Gian Francesco Albani was born at Urbino on July 23, 1649. At the time of his election he had not yet taken religious orders and he only accepted after insistent urging by the Sacred College. Absolutely contrary to nepotism he was a man of great spiritual and moral stature. He opposed and condemned the Jansenist theories and established moral penalties too for those who did not accept the condemnation. In politics Clement did not perform brilliantly and his interventions were not favored by fortune. He tried to mediate between Louis XIV and Leopold of Hapsburg in the matter of the Spanish succession but his words went unheeded. He did not manage to successfully oppose Amadeo of Savoy who occupied the Kingdom of Sicily and was ready to swallow up the pontifical territories as well. He got into serious conflict with the Emperor Joseph I which ended in war in 1708. Regarding the care and protection of Rome's artistic heritage, he made laws for the first time that prohibited, among other things, anyone from taking any work of art out of the city. Furthermore he established in Rome and Bologna two academies of painting and sculpture. By his own wish Clement was buried under the pavement of the choir in St. Peter's Basilica.

244. INNOCENT XIII (1721-1724)

He was born Michelangelo Conti at Poli (Latium) on May 13, 1655. He belonged to the same family as Popes Innocent III, Gregory IX and Alexander IV. His health did not permit him to devote himself to his ministry with all the energy and commitment that he would have liked. He was effectively helped by his brother Bernardo Maria whom he made cardinal. He reaffirmed the condemnation of the Jansenist ideas. With great determination he acted to discipline the Spanish Church and the Jesuits who were both tempted to become autonomous of Rome and to seek power. He invested Charles VI with the Kingdom of Naples and Sicily, but was not able to obtain recognition of his feudal rights. He also concerned himself with the finances of the Pontifical State by imposing a wise policy of economizing. He loved and fostered arts and letters.

245. BENEDICT XIII (1724-1730)

Pietro Francesco Orsini was born at Gravina on February 2, 1649. He renounced his hereditary rights of primogeniture to become a Dominican friar. A brilliant preacher, he was made cardinal at 23 and pope at 75. He accepted his election out of "obedience", continuing to wear his monk's habit and practise its customs. What most interested him was his spiritual ministry. In fact, he spent all of his time performing sacred rites and pastoral activities, things he also required of the clerics at his side. But the political and administrative aspects of his office he saw as stumbling blocks. Thus he entrusted the temporal government of the Church to Cardinal NiccolÚ Coscia in whom he had great trust, trust which the cardinal did not deserve. Coscia decreed harsh rules for clerics going so far as to imprison transgressors, whereas his friends could do as they pleased with impunity and enriched themselves shamefully. Benedict confirmed the condemnation of the Jansenist doctrine and had the satisfaction of seeing it die out. He called the Holy Year of 1725.

246. CLEMENT XII (1730-1740)

Lorenzo Corsini was born in Florence on April 7, 1652. He began his ecclesiastical career at a late age and was elected pope at 78. Because of his fragile health which often kept him bedridden and incipient blindness which at the end became total, he had his nephew Neri Corsini help him. Neri, on the whole, was worthy of this trust. The first act of his pontificate was an act of justice: he punished Cardinal Coscia and those who wrongly had enriched themselves thanks to him. In so doing they had taken advantage of the naivety and good faith of Pope Benedict XIII. Cardinal Coscia was sentenced to ten years in prison and his possessions all distributed to the poor. On the grounds that anyone could do what he liked with his own money, Clement regulated the lottery which he had made legal again after its prohibition by Benedict XIII. The game was under the administration of the Apostolic Chamber and the proceeds were to go to charity and financing public works. He gave heavy financial support to Venice and Poland in their war against the Turks. He was the first pope to issue a bull condemning the Masons - a secret society originating in England - and calling it heterodox. Even today the Church does not approve of it. He was much concerned for the evangelizing of oriental peoples and intensified the missionary work in those parts. He opened the Capitoline museums to the public, had the famous Trevi Fountain built and began work on the facade of the basilica of St. John Lateran where he is buried.

247. BENEDICT XIV (1740-1758)

He was born Prospero Lambertini in Bologna on March 31, 1675 and began his ecclesiastical career at a very early age, quickly rising to the highest offices due to his brilliance and vast culture. The conclave that elected him lasted six months but made a good choice: it fell upon a very balanced man, a moderate of great piety who attentively protected orthodoxy, a lover and patron of the arts and an excellent politician. These qualities made everyone love him during his lifetime and kept his memory alive for very long after his death. Even non-Catholics liked him. He encountered the problem of the Enlightenment and the absolutism of the Christian states with great tolerance. He granted many benefits and sometimes sacrificed his own. He called the famous Holy Year of 1750 and was very active in regard to ecclesiastical discipline and religious practise. Sometimes he made important decisions, abolishing, for example, the Inquisition in Tuscany, condemning secret and clandestine societies and the obscene press. He also outlawed duelling, vehemently proclaimed matrimony indissoluble and ordered Chinese Christians to abandon pagan rites that bordered on superstition. His shrewd and fair fiscal policy succeeded in setting the public accounts straight to the point of accumulating a surplus that was earmarked for public works. He did not practise nepotism but tried to help everyone and favor the interests of all the various parties. He made maximum use of the art of mediation, founded several art academies and established prizes to stimulate students. He restored many Roman monuments, the Colosseum among them.

248. CLEMENT XIII (1758-1769)

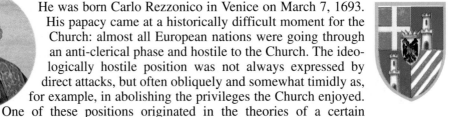

He was born Carlo Rezzonico in Venice on March 7, 1693. His papacy came at a historically difficult moment for the Church: almost all European nations were going through an anti-clerical phase and hostile to the Church. The ideologically hostile position was not always expressed by direct attacks, but often obliquely and somewhat timidly as, for example, in abolishing the privileges the Church enjoyed. One of these positions originated in the theories of a certain Nicholas von Hontheim who, writing under the pseudonym of Phebronius, spread ideas regarding the limitations of papal power in favor of national churches. Monasteries and religious orders were suppressed, clerical powers limited and privileges and immunities cancelled. The pope protested energetically against all these provisions and defended the age-old rights of the Church. All in vain. He supported another cause in his own person: producing numerous documents on various occasions he defended the Jesuits who were at the time being persecuted and systematically expelled from all the Catholic countries, including the Papal State. Within ten years the order was abolished in Portugal, France and Spain and their colonies in Latin America and the Kingdom of the Two Sicilies. Clement called all to an assembly at Civitavecchia and promulgated a constitution in their favor. He achieved nothing. As Sixtus V had already done, he tried to sanitize the malaria-afflicted Pontine Marshes and he completed the work on the Trevi Fountain.

249. CLEMENT XIV (1769-1774)

Vincenzo Antonio Ganganelli was born at Sant'Arcangelo near Rimini on October 31, 1705. The conclave was divided into those who favored and those who opposed the suppression of the Jesuits. A worthy, upright person who totally against nepotism, Clement was elected after formally vowing not to favor the Jesuits. So great was the uproar over the question and so insistent and dogged the opposition to the Jesuits that Clement was compelled to abolish the order. Twenty four thousand people had to go over to the secular clergy. They were expelled from almost all European countries and found shelter only in Russia and Prussia where they gathered and remained until the order was reconstituted under Pius VII. Forcing this decision was were the lay forces of the entire world and, above all, the three Bourbon crowns of France, Spain and Naples. In exchange for this sacrifice Clement won some advantages: Louis XV's commitment to fight anti-religious propaganda, the condemnation of Voltaire's works and the restitution of Benevento, Avignon and Venassino. He founded the Clementine Museum in the Vatican which today is fused with that of Pius, and he fostered continuing work on sanitization of the Pontine Marshes. He prohibited the ignominious practice of mutilating the singers of the Sistine Chapel, the famous castratos. He died in a very mysterious way so that there was talk of poisoning in which fingers inevitably were pointed at the Jesuits.

250. PIUS VI (1775-1799)

Giovanni Angelo Braschi was born at Cesena in Romagna on December 25, 1717. Like Clement XIV, he too had to promise never to reconstitute the Company of Jesus. He practised a moderate amount of nepotism, compensating for this defect with his distinct love of culture and the arts, with his amiable ways and with an honest, sincerely religious life even if he tended towards opulent show and frivolity. If he started his reign a little frivolously, towards the end he displayed courage and even heroism. His first significant act as pope was to call the Holy Year of 1775. But after the first quiet years things changed. Pius VI had to confront two events of extraordinary historical importance: the French revolution and the imperious rise of Napoleon. Both events created problems and suffering for the Church. The revolution, condemned by the pope, was clearly anti-clerical and persecuted the Church and the priests. Napoleon, on the other hand, represented a real threat to the survival of the Papal State. In fact, he used a pretext in order to destroy it. First of all, he forced the pope to sign the humiliating Treaty of Tolentino renouncing the possession of Avignon, Venassino, Bologna, Ferrara and all of Romagna as well as agreeing to pay an enormous sum - 31 million! - and cede many precious art works. Secondly, he took advantage of an incident regarding his ambassador to invade Rome with an army, declared the temporal power of the popes finished and even took Pius VI prisoner, deporting him to France. The pope arrived there, after a long and painful circuitous route, very ill and in a stretcher. At 82 the trip had been an interminable calvary. In fact, he died after just a few days. By Napoleon's wish his remains were returned to Rome and buried in the Vatican Grottoes.

251. PIUS VII (1800-1823)

He was born Barnaba Chiaramonti at Cesena in Romagna on April 14, 1742. A conclave elected him pope that was held in Venice under the protection of Austria, but he could not immediately enter Rome because of a hostile atmosphere provoked by Napoleon's upheaval of the situation. The beginning was very hard for him. But thanks to his diplomatic ability, Pius VII was able to stipulate a concordat with France and even to become Napoleon's friend. According to this concordat France had the right to nominate bishops and the Holy See only to confirm them. Admittedly it was a long step backwards, but at least the Catholic faith once more became the major religion in France. At the conclusion of the treaty the pope crowned Napoleon Bonaparte in the cathedral of Notre Dame in Paris. But the peace was of short duration. With his lust for power, Napoleon occupied the territories of the Papal State. The pope protested and excommunicated him. So Napoleon entered Rome, declared the end of the pope's temporal power and took Pius VII off to France as a prisoner. He forced him to sign a concordat which the pope later disavowed. Pius's troubles ended in the same year when Napoleon lost power and was exiled to the island of Elba. In 1815 the Vienna Congress reconstituted the Papal State. The air of restoration which Europe breathed unfortunately influenced Pius VII in a way to make him establish an authoritarian, anti-libertarian regime. One of his following acts was to re-establish the Company of Jesus. He created the noble guards and a new flag with the white and yellow colors which remain even today. Pius VII did much to beautify Rome. He had Valadier do up the famous Piazza del Popolo surmounted by the Pincio Park and founded the Chiaramonti Museum in the Vatican. He was unable to celebrate the Holy Year of 1800 and died at 82 from a banal accident.

252. LEO XII (1823-1829)

Annibale Sermattei della Genga was born at the Genga Castle near Ancona on August 22, 1760. A good and extremely charitable man, he began his pontificate by distributing money to the poor, providing dowries for 100 poor girls selected at random and reclaiming many pawned objects from the Monte di Pietà for their owners. He followed careful, parsimonious economic policies which reduced expenses and so led to the abolition of some taxes. He fought successfully against banditry. Relations with other states were given particular care, favoring concordats which allowed the local churches to reorganize. In opposition to these virtues there was a shadow side: he was extremely conservative and opposed to any least hint of liberal ideas. In fact, he hanged quite a number of people without thinking twice, not only ordinary criminals but also some who were followers of new ideas. He got rid of laymen from administrative offices and put clerics in their places with the aim of strengthening the congregations. He persecuted and condemned secret societies, including the political secret society of the Carbonari. Among so many negative attitudes there was one surprizing incongruity: he took Gallileo's writings off the index of prohibited books. He began the work of reconstruction on the basilica of San Paolo fuori le mura which had been destroyed by fire in 1823. He was not a pope whom the people loved, perhaps because of his ultra-conservatism. On the contrary, he was much criticized and taken as a target by Rome's famous talking statues.

253. PIUS VIII (1829-1830)

He was born Francesco Saverio Castiglioni at Cingoli on November 20, 1761. He too, when he was bishop of Montalto, had the experience of dealing with the overbearing Napoleon who tried to force him to make a vow of fidelity. He resisted courageously, but the price of refusing was to be confined in another city. A good and honest man, absolutely opposed to nepotism, once elected he forbade his relatives to leave their home town and to change their life styles and standard of living. He had to face problems of all kinds, not least the revolutionary movements which were making their first threatening appearances in Romagna and Rome. He took a moderately liberal approach to them contrary to Leo XII's. He was in fact convinced, and said so, that the only way of overcoming these serious problems was to be mild and charitable, persuasive and conciliatory. Nevertheless he fought secret associations and societies, but moderately and not fanatically. He himself gave greater liberty to English Catholics. Despite his many humane qualities he was not loved by the Roman people.

254. GREGORY XVI (1834-1846)

Bartolomeo Alberto Cappellari was born at Belluno on September 18, 1765. Libertarian revolutions and insurrections by now were breaking out everywhere, including the Papal State. Gregory, who was absolutely conservative and anti-liberal immediately emanated repressive laws against the new ideas, enrolled a militia of voluntaries to oppose the rebels and did not hesitate to call on Austria and France for help. He called on all, including the clergy, for discipline and submission, demanding that they abandon all aspirations and actions that went against the constituted order. He also published an encyclical on the subject in which he banned freedom of the press. For all these reasons he was harshly criticized by liberals. Nevertheless he was a good governor of the Church, absolutist but not tyrannical. He tried to improve the living conditions of the Jews relegated to the ghetto; abolished the list of citizens who had not observed the Easter precept and he lowered the age of majority from 25 to 21. He commissioned many public works, rectified the Aniene River in many points, improved the mouth of the Tiber and the port of Civitavecchia. He also continued the reconstruction of San Paolo fuori le mura, expanded the Vatican buildings and founded the Etruscan and Egyptian museums. He fostered archeological studies, favoring the digs in the Roman forum and the catacombs.

255. PIUS IX (1846-1878)

He was born Giovanni Maria Mastai Ferretti at Senegallia in the Marches on May 13, 1792. A virtuous and cultured man he had the reputation of being liberal in his ideas and tendencies. The first things he did as pope confirmed the expectations of those who saw him as open to the new ideas that were gaining ground. As soon as he was elected he declared an amnesty for political crimes and then established the *Consulta* which was a government of popular representatives that guaranteed more freedom to citizens and to the press. He went so far as to send troops to Lombardy in support of the Piedmontese troops fighting their first war of independence. But enthusiasm for him was extinguished when it became clear that Pius IX was indeed ready to make some concessions along humanitarian and social lines, but not to dismantle the Papal State nor to renounce temporal power which, he liked to say, was "not his" and hence not his to give up. In 1848 the first riots broke out in Rome too and the pope, disguised as a simple priest, had to flee to Gaeta under the protection of the Bourbons. In Rome a republic was proclaimed that was very short-lived. The French, Austrians and Bourbons reconquered it and returned it to the pope who settled there again with less liberal intentions. From that moment on all his acts had only one aim: to save the Papal State. His subsequent acts of government both political and religious - the promulgation of the dogma of the Immaculate Conception, the convening of the Ecumenical Council Vatican I and the dogma of the infallibility of the pope - aside from their strict meaning as doctrine, were also political and intended to strengthen the prestige and the person of the pontiff. Still, he did not succeed in bringing events to a halt: the Papal State dwindled progressively until it was reduced practically to St. Peter's Basilica and the Vatican buildings and gardens. The Vatican I Council was still in session when the Italian troops entered Rome and put an end to the temporal power of the popes that had lasted more than a thousand years. Pius IX closed himself within the Vatican walls refusing all contact with the new kingdom of Italy - in fact, he excommunicated the king - and lived in isolation. He died at 86 after a reign of 32 years, a record which no other pope has yet beaten.

256. LEO XIII (1873-1903)

Vincenzo Gioacchino Pecci was born at Carpineto near Anagni in Latium on March 2, 1810 and was elected by a very short conclave lasting hardly two days. The situation he inherited from Pius IX was grave and heavy: after many centuries the Roman pontiff had lost temporal power and with it a good part of his religious and political influence. The changed conditions required a rethinking and working out of the role of the pope and the church in the context of the new political and social realities. It was necessary to reestablish contact with the State that had been so brusquely interrupted by Pius IX. Immediately upon his election he blessed the people as was customary, not from the loggia outside in the traditional way, but from within St. Peter's Basilica. This act, interpreted as a sign of closure, earned him much criticism and brought on a wave of anti-clericalism. His was true closure: Pope Leo, in fact, took a very hard attitude full of resentment towards the Italian State. He forbade Catholics to take part in any political and civil activity of national life, thus causing them much conflict of conscience and no little suffering. The program he set himself was an ambitious one: to return the Church to its ancient spiritual grandeur. Thus he set to work to recuperate the prestige, authority and salvational function of the Church, and for the pope the role of spiritual guide that Christ had bestowed upon him. His international activity became very intense and, thanks to the exchanges he promoted, he acquired a more direct and real knowledge of the new problems people were experiencing in post-revolutionary and post-libertarian modern industrial society. These problems regarded work, exploitation, freedom and the purity of the faith. He tried to provide an answer to them by proposing a social doctrine based on the principles of the Gospels. Of particular importance was his encyclical *Rerum novarum* from which he began and developed the thought of the Church concerning the social policy towards work. He was the first pope to be filmed. He called the Holy Year of 1900 as a token of pacification.

257. PIUS X, ST. (1903-1914)

Giuseppe Sarto was born at Riese near Treviso on June 2, 1835. Conservative in his religious ideas, he counterbalanced this doctrinal rigor with a generous and cordial openness to all that could also be extroverted and nonconformist. He never forgot his obligation to the poor to whom he always showed charity. His extreme conservatism led him to oppose and condemn any idea of democracy especially when it called itself "Christian", seeing in it a form of anarchy and rebellion against the constituted order. This characteristic alienated many people. His directness was seen by some to be dangerous, especially among the Curia. And it was precisely the Curia, which ought to have collaborated with him in governing the Church, that made problems for him due to a different way of seeing things. Therefore he began decisively to reform the ecclesiastical structure by putting emphasis on the discipline and education of the clergy. He wrote and promulgated the famous catechism which is addressed primarily to children to whom he personally gave lessons in doctrine on Sundays. He drew up a new Codex of Canon Law and ordered the periodic publication of a volume called *Acta Apostolicae Sedis* in which the papal laws and dispositions were promulgated - in effect, the old Decretals of Gregory IX (no.178). He condemned so-called Modernism and all the innovations aimed at changing the social status quo, thus arousing discontent and enmity everywhere. Compared with his predecessors he was more conciliatory towards the Italian state and, among other things, removed the ban for Catholics on participation in public life. He tried in every possible way to smother World War I which broke out in 1914. He showed his consistency of character when he refused the request of Emperor Franz Joseph to bless his troops, saying: "I only bless peace". Pius X died soon afterwards - some say of heartbreak for the tragedy of the war - as poor as he had lived.

258. BENEDICT XV (1914-1922)

Giacomo della Chiesa was born at Genoa Pegli on November 21, 1854. His was not an open personality but he was a tireless worker who was called upon to lead the Church during the tragic first world war. He was concerned with being the peacemaker. He constantly urged peace, was never heeded and sometimes misunderstood, especially when he called the war "a useless massacre". Thus he took no one's side and this created hostility and resentment against him. He was, however, prodigious in helping war victims: the Vatican became a center for information and requests of all kinds. But his concern about the war did not make him forget the work of governing the Church. He condemned Modernism as had Pius X. He founded the Congregation for the Eastern Churches and Milan's Sacred Heart University. He favored Italy's Partito Popolare and Christian unionism in all countries. He established more normal relations with the Italian state as well as new diplomatic relations with France and intensified those with England which once again had representatives in the Vatican after three and a half centuries. He died of bronchial pneumonia.

259. PIUS XI (1922-1939)

He was born Achille Ratti at Desio near Milan on May 31, 1857. As pope he returned to the old tradition of blessing the Roman people and the world from the balcony of St. Peter's which Pius IX had interrupted following the annexation of Rome by the new kingdom of Italy. This gesture was appreciated, especially by Italy which was ready to reconsider relations with the Holy See so that in February 1929 the new Lateran pact was signed. Thanks to this treaty the Vatican City state was established: autonomous, independent, with its own territory and laws. The Vatican recognized the kingdom of Italy while Italy, in turn, recognized the Vatican state under the sovereignty of the Roman pontiff. Pius IX was a good politician and diplomat but intransigent with regard to doctrine. In memorable encyclicals he took his distance from and condemned Communism, Fascism and Nazism. He did not succeed in lifting the persecutions of the Church and the clergy in some countries such as Russia, Mexico and Spain. He fostered missionary work and greatly stimulated Catholic culture by establishing various universities in all parts of the world. He helped to promote Catholic Action and defended it from all attacks. He called two Holy Years, one in 1925 and a special one in 1933 on the occasion of the 19th centenary of the Redemption. Of exceptional historical importance for that time was the setting up of Vatican Radio, an idea thought up by Guglielmo Marconi. The voice of the pope was heard throughout the world. His first message was broadcast in Italian.

260. PIUS XII (1939-1958)

Eugenio Pacelli was born in Rome on March 2, 1876. He was unanimously elected on March 2, 1939, his birthday. After a few months World War II broke out during which the pope performed an invaluable service of information and assistance, just as Benedict XV had done during World War I. He organized a vast program of humanitarian aide in favor of whomever needed it: Jews, opponents of totalitarian regimes and, finally, of Germans after their defeat. Many people were saved from persecution on both sides. Once the war was over his pastoral activity was taken up with the fight against Marxism which he condemned, excommunicating its followers. He gave a conservative stamp to his government. During the Holy Year of 1950 he proclaimed the dogma of the Assumption into heaven of the Most Blessed Virgin. It was he who began the popular tradition whereby every December 8 the pope goes to bless the statue of Mary Immaculate in Piazza di Spagna in Rome. By his order too the excavations under St. Peter's Basilica were undertaken by the archeologist Guarducci who finally found the tomb of St. Peter. What the age-old tradition of the Church had always maintained could now be demonstrated by scientific arguments. He was untiring in his pastoral activities, even when gravely ill.

261. JOHN XXIII (1958-1963)

He was born Angelo Giuseppe Roncalli at Sotto il Monte near Bergamo on November 25, 1881. His election appeared to be the fruit of a compromise between the traditionalist and progressive factions. As such it was supposed to have a provisional character. But John turned out to be anything but a transitional pope, leaving on the Church the mark of a new way of being. He stepped down from the pedestal on which the people had always seen the pope installed and drew near to them showing real interest in their problems and sufferings. He left the Vatican to visit the ill and the incarcerated without observing any rules or formalities. He would stop and talk to the common people and workers, and was fond of saying that work offered to God was in itself a prayer. He acted outside all categories and frames of reference as when he received the son-in-law of Nikita Krushchev the head of Russian and world Communism without worrying about the opposition of the Curia and the excommunication Pius XII had pronounced on him. The people immediately understood the change of direction and gave him in exchange a degree of affection and enthusiasm never before seen. On the level of doctrine, he took up again and developed the Church's ideas on social policy while calling the attention of the nations to the urgency of creating a world climate of peace. But his name is mostly connected to the calling of Vatican Council II to everyone's great surprize. The grave problems the world was experiencing at that time together with those within the Church - the drop in religious vocations and the uneasiness of the ecclesiastical world in its contacts with the new problems - all of this was in urgent need of new solutions. The Council, at whose first session Pope John was present, responded to these. John died only a few months later of a tumor, mourned by all, in particular by the Roman populace that kept vigil all through the night in St. Peter's Square praying for his soul. Everyone still refers to him as "the good pope".

262. PAUL VI (1963-1978)

Giovanni Battista Montini was born at Concesio near Brescia on September 26, 1897. In the footsteps of John XXIII, he continued to interpret the pope's role as being constantly more deeply immersed in social reality in the midst of the people with whom he loved having direct contact, even if he was not endowed with the same immediacy and likeability of his predecessor. His movements outside the Vatican and his trips far from Rome - he visited many countries of the world - are the testimony of this new way of conceiving the universal salvational mission of the Church and the pope. His recurring themes were peace among the peoples and social justice. Immediately after his election he brought Vatican II to a close. He stamped the new conciliatory spirit with his action as pastor of the Church. The themes of his daily work were ecumenicism, relations with other religions, the phenomenon of atheism and the problem of the inner reform of the Church. The particular attention he reserved for the existential unease of modern man with his doubts and weaknesses and the brotherly understanding he showed aroused some criticism, but they made him a symbol of a church that questions and suffers. Some of his positions, that alternated between conservative and progressive, seemed surprising and earned him the label of indecisive and contradictory. For example, a part of the American press called him "a dangerous Communist" on one occasion. He took a clear stand against divorce, abortion and in favor of celibacy for priests. He was greatly upset by the rebellion of the French Bishop Lefevre who contested all the post-council renewal and Paul called him to order a number of times but never punished him. He also called the Holy Year of 1975 and decided on the reform of the Curia, introducing new rules for conclaves to rejuvenate it, make it more efficient and more international. He increased the number of non-Italian cardinals in the Sacred College ordering that a part of them should come from Third World countries. Furthermore he prescribed that they leave office at the age of 80. However much absorbed as he was by serious world problems, he did not neglect the arts and founded the Vatican Museum for religious and modern art. He also financed the construction of the famous Nervi Hall for papal audiences. He is buried in the Vatican Grottoes in a simple tomb underground as he himself stipulated.

263. JOHN PAUL I (1978)

Albino Luciani was born at Canale d'Agordo near Belluno on October 17, 1912. Pope Paul VI named him patriarch of Venice and later cardinal. During one of Paul VI's visits to Venice he placed his stole on Luciani's shoulders. This event was tenderly recalled by John Paul I in his brief address from the balcony of St. Peter's following his election. It had been interpreted as a sign of Paul VI's desire and of his predilection for Luciani. A simple soul and modest in his ways like a parish priest, he was called "the smiling pope". With regard to doctrine his position was clear and traditional. As a cardinal, for example, he was firmly against divorce and dissolved some Catholic organizations in his diocese that had taken a pro-divorce position. In the same way he was inflexible towards dissenting Catholics. There was only one faith and Catholics had to follow the directives of the Church authorities. As pope his pre-announced program was prayer, discipline within the Church and fidelity to the Vatican II Council. Humble and simple, he did not betray his origins and his ideas when elevated to the papacy: in fact, he refused the gestatorial chair and the tiara, the symbols of earthly power, nor did he want to be crowned. His success was immediate and general, but very brief - only 33 days. His sudden death from a heart attack was a great blow that took everyone by surprise and led to fantastic conjectures. Even today it is said that he barely had time to give the world a glimpse of what the style of his pontificate would be, but that was enough to arouse enthusiasm and hope and win him a place in the hearts of all.

264. JOHN PAUL II (1978 -)

Karol Wojtyla was born at Wadowice in Poland on May 18, 1920. A brilliant student and busy in pastoral activities, especially among the workers and young people, Paul VI named him bishop of Krakow and then cardinal. He was the first non-Italian pope elected since the Dutch Hadrian VI in 1522 (no. 218). Like John Paul I, he too refused to be crowned with the tiara. With regard to him, who continues to govern the Church authoritatively, one can indicate some personality traits and some of the events which have been distinguishing marks of his papacy. A charismatic personality par excellence, he has the natural gift of immediately gripping people who respond in great numbers to his call. Crowds of hundreds of thousands always congregate when John Paul II appears. He has a predilection for the young whom he spurs to seek out and be witness to Christianity. He has stamped his mission with the mark of charity, with continuous interchanges and personal relationships, but also with the spreading of the Christian message to whose values he has repeatedly recalled the peoples, especially the European ones. As bishop of Rome he has made a habit of apostolic visits to the parishes of the diocese, while as pastor of the universal Church he has made his voice heard and has gone to visit the Christians of the five continents. He has expertly exploited modern technology and communication media, raising them to the level of fully qualified tools of evangelization. The attempt made on his life in St. Peter's

Square on May 13, 1981 during one of his audiences dealt a hard blow to his inexhaustible dynamism, but it did not stop him. Wojtyla adamantly refused to slow down. In the field of doctrine he strongly reaffirmed the value and the continuing validity of traditional Christian teachings to which all Catholics must conform, ignoring fashions and experiments. For the purpose of giving the faithful a clear and certain tool of doctrine, he published <<The Catechism of the Catholic Church>>. John Paul II, on the basis of his attitudes and his doctrine, has also been called the pope of "certainties" without yielding and without doubt. More than once he has taken positions against abortion and divorce, against Western societies' consumerism and against the deviation which is Communism. He has been the first pope to allow lay employees of the Vatican to organize into labor unions. His faith, composed of rigorous and sometimes harsh principles, is sweetened by a tender devotion to the Blessed Virgin Mary whose initial "M" figures in his coat-of-arms. Having celebrated the special Holy Year of the Redemption in 1983, he has for some years been preparing for the Jubilee of the year 2000 which, one can be sure, will leave its mark on the life of Rome and of the Church.

POPE JOAN

It is said that Leo IV was succeeded by a woman, Pope Joan. Fruit of the fervid popular imagination, this legend arose in the Thirteenth Century, inexplicably, like many fantastic medieval stories, and it spread with unusual rapidity. It tells of a woman who, dressed as a man, was elected pope and deceived everyone for two and a half years. The name by which she was known was Giovanni Anglico. But the truth came out due to a chance as naive as it was incredible: during a drive from St. Peter's to St. John Lateran the papal cortege came to a halt near the Colosseum because the pope had to give birth. She delivered the child but soon after was stoned to death. The masquerade as a man began when, long before the election, the young Anglico went to study in Greece and became very learned. On her return to Rome where she was a teacher, she made a career through contact with Pope Leo. By now historical criticism has revealed with total certainty that the story is pure fiction containing not even a grain of truth. But the notoriety and credibility it reached, even on official levels, was enormous. Up until the 16th Century, with few exceptions, no one questioned the truth of Pope Joan's existence. Among other things, it was a recurring point of reference for Protestant polemics against the Roman Church.

THE ELECTION OF THE POPE

From the death of one pope until the election of his successor - a period known as a vacancy - the Church is governed by the deacon of the cardinals, the chamberlain. It is his job to convene the College of Cardinals for the election of a new pontiff within twenty days of the death of the old pope. According to a decree of Paul VI all cardinals can attend who are under the age of 80, beyond which age they can neither elect or be elected. The conclave, from the Latin *cum clave*, (for its origin see pope no.179) is generally held in the Sistine Chapel where the cardinals are kept in rigid isolation with no contact with the outside so as to avoid any and all pressures or influences. At a certain point the doors are closed and the consultations and voting begin. There are three ways in which the pope can be elected: by a vote; by "compromise" in which a group of cardinal proxies are delegated to make the choice whose decision must be accepted; and by "inspiration" when the assembly votes unanimously for a candidate proposed by an elector. Two thirds of the votes are enough to elect. The results of each balloting are communicated to the public gathered in St. Peter's Square by means of the well-known "smoke signals" produced by a stove in which the ballots are burned after each voting. This operation takes place in a room next to the Sistine Chapel. If the smoke is black, no pope has been elected (this is achieved by adding damp straw to the ballots); if the smoke is white (only the ballots are burned) the election has taken place. The smoke comes out of a chimney situated on the roof of the Sistine Chapel. Once the elected has accepted and has chosen his name, he receives the "act of obedience" from all the cardinals who prostrate themselves before him and kiss his foot. Once all the rites and formalities have been performed, the announcement is made "Habemus papam" - "We have a pope" and the new pontiff appears on the balcony of St. Peter's facade from where he makes the apostolic blessing "urbi et orbi" - "to the city of Rome and to the world" - to Rome of which he is bishop and to the world of which he is the universal pastor. During the first centuries the pope was elected by the clergy and the Roman people. When the papacy began to take on an ever more political importance, other forces outside the Church were impelled to try to determine or at least influence the outcome of the election of the pope to their own advantage. These ran from the Byzantine emperor to the Holy Roman emperor to the kings of France, Spain and Germany and the ever-present Roman patrician families. For centuries the two empires had the right to confirm the elected pope which meant they had a recognized faculty of control. The component that disappeared most rapidly was that of the people.

CHRONOLOGICAL LIST
OF THE POPES AND ANTI-POPES

The names of the anti-popes are in italics

Peter, St. (64)
Linus, St. (67 - 76)
Cletus Or Anacletus, St. (76 - 88)
Clement I, St. (88 - 97)
Evaristus, St. (97 - 105)
Alexander I, St. (105 - 115)
Sixtus I, St. (115 - 125)
Telesphorus, St. (125 - 136)
Hyginus, St. (136 - 140)
Pius I, St. (140 - 155)
Anicetus I, St. (155 - 166)
Soter, St. (166 - 175)
Eleutherius, St. (175 - 189)
Victor I, St. (189 - 199)
Zephyrinus, St. (199 - 217)
Callistus, St. (217 - 222)
Hippolytus (217 - 235)
Urban I, St. (222 - 230)
Pontian, St. (230 - 235)
Anterus, St. (235 - 236)
Fabian, St. (236 - 250)
Cornelius, St. (251 - 253)
Novation (251 - 258)
Lucius I, St. (253 - 254)
Stephen I, St. (254 - 257)
Sixtus II, St. (257 - 258)
Dionysius, St. (259 - 268)
Felix I, St. (269 - 274)
Eutychian, St. (275 - 283)
Gaius Or Caius, St. (283 - 296)
Marcellinus St. (296 - 304)
Marcellus I, St. (308 - 309)
Eusebius, St. (309)
Miltiades (311 - 314)
Silvester I, St. (314 - 335)
Mark, St. (336)
Julius I, St. (337 - 352)
Liberius (352 - 366)
Felix II (355 - 365)
Damasus I, St. (366 - 384)
Ursinus (366 - 367)
Siricius, St. (384 - 399)
Anastasius I, St. (399 - 401)
Innocent I, St. (401 - 417)
Zosimus, St. (417 - 418)
Eulalius (418 - 419)
Boniface I, St. (418 - 422)

Celestine I, St. (422 - 432)
Sixtus III, St. (432 - 440)
Leo I, St. (440 - 461)
Hilarus, St. (461 - 468)
Simplicius, St. (468 - 483)
Felix III, St. (483 - 492)
Gelasius I, St. (492 - 496)
Anastasius II, St. (496 - 498)
Symmachus, St. (498 - 514)
Lawrence (498 - 499; 501 - 506)
Hormisdas, St. (514 - 523)
John I, St. (523 - 526)
Felix IV, St. (526 - 530)
Dioscurus (530)
Boniface II (530 - 532)
John II (533 - 535)
Agapitus I, St. (535 - 536)
Silverius, St. (536 - 537)
Vigilius (537 - 555)
Pelagius I (556 - 561)
John Iii (561 - 574)
Benedict I (575 - 579)
Pelagius II (579 - 590)
Gregory I, St. (590 - 604)
Sabinian (604 - 606)
Boniface III (607)
Boniface IV (608 - 615)
Adeodatus I, St. (615 - 618)
Boniface V (619 - 625)
Honorius I (625 - 638)
Severinus (640)
John IV (640 - 642)
Theodore I (642 - 649)
Martin I, St. (649 - 655)
Eugene I, St. (654 - 657)
Vitalian, St. (657 - 672)
Adeodatus II (672 - 676)
Donus (676 - 678)
Agatho, St. (678 - 681)
Leo II, St. (682 - 683)
Benedict II, St. (684 - 685)
John V (685 - 686)
Conon (686 - 687)
Theodore (687)
Paschal (687)
Sergius I, St. (687 - 701)
John VI (701-705)

John VII (705 - 707)
Sissinius (708)
Constantine (708 - 715)
Gregory II, St. (715 - 731)
Gregory III, St. (731 - 741)
Zacharias, St. (741 - 752)
Stephen II (III) (752 - 757)
Paul I, St. (757 - 767)
Costantine (767 - 768)
Philipe (768)
Stephen III (IV) (768 - 772)
Hadrian I (772 - 795)
Leo III, St. (795 - 816)
Stephen IV (V) (816 - 817)
Paschal I, St. (817 - 824)
Eugene II (824 - 827)
Valentine (827)
Gregory IV (827 - 844)
Iohn (844)
Sergius II (844 - 847)
Leo IV, St. (847 - 855)
Benedict III (855 - 858)
Anastasius (855)
Nicholas I, St. (858 - 867)
Hadrian II (867 - 872)
John VIII (872 - 882)
Marinus I (882 - 884)
Hadrian III, St. (884 - 885)
Stephen V (VI) (885 - 891)
Formosus (891 - 896)
Boniface VI (896)
Stephen VI (896 - 897)
Romanus (897)
Theodore II (897)
John IX (898 - 900)
Benedict IV (900 - 903)
Leo V (903)
Christopher (903 - 904)
Sergius III (904 - 911)
Anasatsius III (911 - 913)
Lando (913 - 914)
John X (914 - 928)
Leo VI (928)
Stephen VII (VIII) (928 - 931)
John XI (931 - 935)
Leo VII (936 - 939)
Stephen VIII (IX) (939 - 942)

Marinus II (942 - 946)
Agapitus II (946 - 955)
John XII (955 - 964)
Leo VIII (963 - 965)
Benedict V (964 - 966)
John XIII (965 - 972)
Benedict VI (973 - 974)
Boniface VII (974; 984 - 985)
Benedict VII (974 - 983)
John XIV (983 - 984)
John XV (985 - 996)
Gregory V (996 - 999)
John XVI (997 - 998)
Silvester II (999 - 1003)
John XVII (1003)
John XVIII (1004 - 1009)
Sergius IV (1009 - 1012)
Benedict VIII (1012 - 1024)
Gregory (VI) (1012)
John XIX (1024 - 1032)
Benedict IX (1032 - 1044; 1045; 1047 - 1048)
Silvester III (1045)
Gregory VI (1045 - 1046)
Clement II (1046 - 1047)
Damasus II (1048)
Leo IX, St. (1949 - 1054)
Victor II (1055 - 1057)
Stephen IX (X) (1057 - 1058)
Benedict X (1058 - 1059)
Nicholas II (1059 - 1061)
Alexander II (1061 - 1073)
Honorius (II) (1061 - 1064)
Gregory VII, St. (1073 - 1085)
Clement (III) (1080; 1084 - 1100)
Victor III, Bl. (1086 - 1087)
Urban II, Bl. (1088 - 1099)
Paschal II (1099 - 1118)
Theodoric (1100 - 1101)
Albert (1101)
Silvester IV (1105 - 1111)
Gelasius II (1118 - 1119)
Gregory (VIII) (1118 - 1121)
Callistus II (1119 - 1124)
Honorius II (1124 - 1130)
Celestine (II) (1124)
Innocent II (1130 - 1143)
Anacletus II (1130 - 1138)
Victor IV (1138)
Celestine II (1143 - 1144)
Lucius II (1144 - 1145)
Eugene III, Bl. (1145 - 1153)
Anastasius IV (1153 - 1154)
Hadrian IV (1154 - 1159)

Alexander III (1159 - 1181)
Victor IV (1159 - 1164)
Paschal III (1164 - 1168)
Callistus (III) (1168 - 1178)
Innocent (III) (1179 - 1180)
Lucius III (1181 - 1185)
Urban III (1185 - 1187)
Gregory VIII (1187)
Clement III (1187 - 1191)
Celestine III (1191 - 1198)
Innocent III (1198 - 1216)
Honorius III (1216 - 1227)
Gregory IX (1227 - 1241)
Celestine IV (1241)
Innocent IV (1243 - 1254)
Alexander IV (1245 - 1261)
Urban IV (1261 - 1264)
Clement IV (1265 - 1268)
Gregory X, Bl. (1271 - 1276)
Innocent V, Bl. (1276)
Hadrian V (1276)
John XXI (1276 - 1277)
Nicholas III (1277 - 1280)
Martin IV (1281 - 1285)
Honorius IV (1285 - 1287)
Nicholas IV (1288 - 1292)
Celestine V, St. (1294)
Boniface VIII (1295 - 1303)
Benedict XI, Bl. (1303 - 1304)
Clement V (1305 - 1314)
John XXII (1316 - 1334)
Nicholas (V) (1328 - 1330)
Benedict XII (1334 - 1342)
Clement VI (1342 - 1352)
Innocent VI (1352 - 1362)
Urban V, Bl. (1362 - 1370)
Gregory XI (1370 - 1378)
Urban VI (1378 - 1389)
Clement (VII) (1378 - 1394)
Boniface IX (1389 - 1404)
Benedict (XIII) (1394 - 1417)
Innocent VII (1404 - 1406)
Gregory XII (1406 - 1415)
Alexander V (1409 - 1410)
John (XXIII) (1410 - 1415)
Martin V (1417 - 1431)
Clement (VIII) (1423 - 1429)
Benedict (XIV) (1425 - ?)
Eugene IV (1431 - 1447)
Felix V (1439 - 1449)
Nicholas V (1447 - 1455)
Callistus III (1455 - 1458)
Pius II (1458 - 1464)
Paul II (1464 - 1471)

Sixtus IV (1471 - 1484)
Innocent VIII (1484 - 1492)
Alexander VI (1492 - 1503)
Pius III (1503)
Julius II (1503 - 1513)
Leo X (1513 - 1521)
Hadrian VI (1522 - 1523)
Clement VII (1523 - 1534)
Paul III (1534 - 1549)
Julius III (1550 - 1555)
Marcellus II (1555)
Paul IV (1555 - 1559)
Pius IV (1560 - 1565)
Pius V, St. (1566 - 1572)
Gregory XIII (1572 - 1585)
Sixtus V (1585 - 1590)
Urban VII (1590)
Gregory XIV (1590 - 1591)
Innocent IX (1591)
Clement VIII (1592 - 1605)
Leo XI (1605)
Paul V (1605 - 1621)
Gregory XV (1621 - 1623)
Urban VIII (1623 - 1644)
Innocent X (1644 - 1655)
Alexander VII (1655 - 1667)
Clement IX (1667 - 1669)
Clement X (1670 - 1676)
Innocent XI, Bl. (1676 - 1689)
Alexander VIII (1689 - 1691)
Innocent XII (1691 - 1700)
Clement XI (1700 - 1721)
Innocent XIII (1721 - 1724)
Benedict XIII (1724 - 1730)
Clement XII (1730 - 1740)
Benedict XIV (1740 - 1758)
Clement XIII (1758 - 1769)
Clement XIV (1769 - 1774)
Pius VI (1775 - 1799)
Pius VII (1800 - 1823)
Leo XII (1823 - 1829)
Pius VIII (1829 - 1830)
Gregory XVI (1834 - 1846)
Pius IX (1846 - 1878)
Leo XIII (1878 - 1903)
Pius X, St. (1903 - 1914)
Benedict XV (1914 - 1922)
Pius XI (1922 - 1939)
Pius XII (1939 - 1958)
John XXIII (1958 - 1963)
Paul VI (1963 - 1978)
John Paul I (1978)
John Paul II (1978 -   )

ALPHABETICAL INDEX
OF THE POPES

Name	No.	Name	No.	Name	No.
Innocent X	89	Lucius III	60	Sergius IV	48
Innocent XI	91			Severinus	25
Innocent XII	92	Marcellinus	10	Silverius	20
Innocent XIII	92	Marcellus I	10	Silvester I	11
		Marcellus II	83	Silvester II	47
John I	19	Mark	11	Silvester III	50
John II	20	Marinus I	38	Symmachus	18
John III	21	Marinus II	44	Simplicius	17
John IV	25	Martin I	25	Siricius	13
John V	28	Martin IV	67	Sissinius	29
John VI	29	Martin V	75	Sixtus I	3
John VII	29	Miltiades	11	Sixtus II	8
John VIII	37			Sixtus III	15
John IX	40	Nicholas I	37	Sixtus IV	78
John X	42	Nicholas II	52	Sixtus V	85
John XI	43	Nicholas III	67	Soter	4
John XII	44	Nicholas IV	68	Stephen I	8
John XIII	45	Nicholas V	76	Stephen II	32
John XIV	46			Stephen III	33
John XV	47	Paschal I	34	Stephen IV	34
John XVII	48	Paschal II	55	Stephen V	38
John XVIII	48	Paul I	32	Stephen VI	39
John XIX	49	Paul II	77	Stephen VII	43
John XXI	66	Paul III	82	Stephen VIII	43
John XXII	70	Paul IV	83	Stephen IX	52
John XXIII	101	Paul V	88		
John Paul I	102	Paul VI	101	Telesphorus	3
John Paul II	102	Pelagius I	21	Theodore I	25
Julius I	12	Pelagius II	22	Theodore II	40
Julius II	80	Peter	1		
Julius III	83	Pius I	4	Urban I	6
		Pius II	77	Urban II	54
Lando	42	Pius III	79	Urban III	60
Leo I	16	Pius IV	84	Urban IV	64
Leo II	27	Pius V	84	Urban V	72
Leo III	34	Pius VI	95	Urban VI	73
Leo IV	36	Pius VII	96	Urban VII	86
Leo V	41	Pius VIII	97	Urban VIII	89
Leo VI	42	Pius IX	97		
Leo VII	43	Pius X	99	Valentine	35
Leo VIII	45	Pius XI	100	Vigilius	21
Leo IX	51	Pius XII	100	Vitalian	26
Leo X	80	Pontian	6	Victor I	5
Leo XI	87			Victor II	52
Leo XII	96	Romanus	40	Victor III	54
Leo XIII	98				
Liberius	12	Sabinian	23	Zacharias	31
Linus	1	Sergius I	28	Zephyrinus	5
Lucius I	8	Sergius II	36	Zosimus	14
Lucius II	57	Sergius III	41		